W9-BZV-547

Why Faith Is a Virtue

Why Faith Is a Virtue

PHILIP D. SMITH

To Julie Green — a hardworking student and dependable person. There are lots of arguments here, but you can track them all. Taking logic was a happy decision after all. ☺

Phil Smith

CASCADE *Books* · Eugene, Oregon

WHY FAITH IS A VIRTUE

Cascade Books
An Imprint of Wipf and Stock Publishers
199 W. 8th Ave., Suite 3
Eugene, OR 97401

www.wipfandstock.com

ISBN 13: 978-1-62032-691-6

Cataloguing-in-Publication Data

Smith, Philip D.

    Why faith is virtue / Philip D. Smith.

    x + 172 p. ; 23 cm. Includes bibliographical references.

    ISBN 13: 978-1-62032-691-6

    1. Ethics. 2. Virtue. 3. MacIntyre, Alasdair C. I. Title.

BJ1012 .S655 2014

Manufactured in the U.S.A.

In memory of Lela Morrill, minister of good news,

and my parents, A. K. Smith and Beverly J. Smith,
who learned much of faith from Lela.

All these people were still living by faith when they died.
They did not receive the things promised; they only saw them and
welcomed them from a distance . . .

—Hebrews 11: 13

Contents

Acknowledgments

This book is dedicated to the memory of Lela Morrill and my parents, A. K. Smith and Beverly J. Smith. Lela was a Quaker minister in the Friends Church in East Wenatchee, Washington, just up the street from our house when I began grade school. By natural births, adoptions, and giving foster care, my parents supplied me with 22 brothers and sisters before I left for college—and one more was added later, when they adopted my brother's daughter after his death. Lela Morrill and my parents showed me what faith looks like in the gritty, imperfect world of real life.

In philosophy I owe most to Arthur Roberts, who was the only philosophy professor at George Fox College when I was a student. Later, Arthur nudged me toward graduate work in philosophy by asking me to teach a History of Philosophy course, when my only preparation had been a course in seminary. I count it a great honor to have succeeded Arthur at George Fox University, though now of course there are three philosophers on faculty.

As chapter 1 makes clear, the theoretical framework of this book is rooted in the work of Robert Adams and Alasdair MacIntyre. From them I adopt the crucial notions of *being for* and virtues in the context of practices. Much of the value of the book lies in these ideas. Nevertheless, readers should not attribute to Adams or MacIntyre any errors I may have made by misconstruing their work.

I have been thinking and writing about the virtue of faith for ten years. In 2007–2008, I was granted a sabbatical by George Fox, during which I drafted most of this book. However, at that time I could find no publisher. By 2009, I was convinced that a key chapter ("What Is Faith?") had serious errors, and I was glad the book had not been published. By 2011, I had discovered the right direction for chapter 2, and in 2012 Wipf and Stock accepted the project.

Peter Boghossian, philosophy professor at Portland State University, disagrees sharply with the theses of this book. Peter says—often, in public lectures—that faith is a "cognitive sickness." Nevertheless, Professor Bog-hossian graciously invited me to give a guest lecture in his Atheism course at PSU on October 25, 2012. That lecture gave me an opportunity to work out much of the content of chapter 2, and questions from some of his students helped me remove some weaknesses.

1

What Is a Virtue?

This book explores the virtue of faith. The exploration will necessarily be incomplete; faith is a far richer topic than can be explicated in a short book. Nevertheless, I hope to say some things that are both true and useful about faith.

Our exploration of faith is philosophical. Notice the word *our*. Philosophy is always, at least implicitly, a conversation. Some philosophers write and speak as if they have a firm and perspicuous grasp of their subject matter; it's possible that some of them actually do. But most of the time most philosophers admit that their work is a contribution to an ongoing activity, often described as a conversation. Philosophers think about complex, confusing, and subtle problems; the sheer difficulty of philosophical problems guarantees that philosophers will make mistakes, with the result that much of their conversation consists in corrections and rebuttals. (Of course, it is also possible that philosophers simply create philosophical problems or make them worse by the way they go about their work. The twentieth-century philosopher Ludwig Wittgenstein thought so.) I wish to make the conversational aspect of philosophy explicit in this book. I intend much of what I say here as an invitation to the reader to join in the exploration of faith.

I said that our exploration of faith is "philosophical." That does *not* mean that I am writing to a guild or to specialists. Quite the contrary, I intend that our exploration of faith, and the invitation to that exploration, be accessible to a wide readership. In this book, technical aspects of the exploration will be kept to a minimum and will always be explained.[1]

In saying that our exploration is philosophical, I *do* mean to exclude appeal to any religious or institutional authority for the positions I urge. Since our topic is the virtue of faith, some readers might expect arguments grounded in Scripture or church dogma. But on my understanding of philosophy (which is widely shared, I think), the philosophical conversation is open to anybody, in the sense that the arguments given and the conclusions recommended are based on generally accessible reasons and evidence. At every stage, the reader is simply invited to judge for herself, by her own lights, whether the argument makes sense.

We aim to explore the virtue of faith. Already, then, we have a specialized term, *virtue*, that needs explanation. In contemporary American speech, *virtue* has suffered a constriction of meaning such that it often means "chastity (esp. in women)," according to one dictionary.[2] Philosophers who write about virtue use the word in a much more general way, something closer to "moral excellence and righteousness; goodness," citing the same dictionary.

So what is a virtue? It's easy to give lists of qualities that have been called virtues at various times.[3] Such lists often overlap—courage, truthfulness, and justice, for example, are almost always included—but sometimes the lists conflict; Aristotle said humility is a vice, while the New Testament treats it as a virtue. A philosophical account of virtue will aim to explain in general terms what a virtue is. Along the way, if it is successful, a philosophical account of virtue will also show why different people have agreed (and disagreed) about particular virtues. Rather than create a list of virtues, in this chapter I will give a general account of virtue. Along the way I will mention various particular virtues in order to illustrate the general account. I assume that most readers will agree that the virtues I use as illustrations really are virtues. But our attention is on the general account rather than the particulars. Of course, there is one virtue I will *not* use as an illustration: the virtue of faith. Some people, particularly philosophers, do not think faith is a virtue, and I will argue in later chapters that it is, so it would beg the question to include faith as one of my examples when I am trying to give a general account of virtue.

1. My remarks in the text do not imply a wholesale criticism of technical work in philosophy. Often philosophical problems require care and precision that can only be achieved with specialized vocabularies, symbolic logic, and the like.

2. *The American Heritage Dictionary*—it was simply the closest to hand when I wrote this chapter.

3. See MacIntyre, *After Virtue*, 181–83, for a comparison of diverse lists of virtues.

Most philosophers who have written about virtues have agreed that they have certain features. First, a virtue is something good about a human being; we sometimes speak of the virtues of a dog, a painting, or a well-ploughed field, but in this book the virtues we wish to understand are characteristics of human beings.

Second, not all good characteristics of a human being count as virtues. Strength, physical beauty, good memory, and visual acuity—these are all talents or traits of persons that are good to have but that we do not count as virtues.[4] We do count things like courage, kindness, patience, and truthfulness as virtues. The difference seems to be this: We *acquire* the virtues, at least to some extent, while natural gifts are simply that, given to us. It seems that I, as a moral agent, am *responsible* to some degree for developing a character of courage and kindness, and I would be blamable if I degenerate or drift into cowardice and cruelty.

Third, virtues endure. Suppose I treat Paul, who works in my office, kindly on one occasion. This hardly makes me a kind person. I might well be a selfish jerk and still treat Paul well on occasion. Virtues, however, are ongoing traits of a person. We can depend on a kind person to act kindly most of the time. Sometimes, of course, a kind person will act "out of character," especially when she is subjected to stress or to unfamiliar situations.[5] But if the virtue is really present, she will return to patterns of behavior in accordance with the virtue.

Fourth, any true account of virtues must leave room for variations in their psychological structure. Some virtues focus on the wellbeing of others, either directly (as with kindness or hospitality) or indirectly (as with civility or politeness[6]). Others, such as courage or self-control, focus on the self, as regulating the self in situations of danger, temptation, or stress. Many virtues require other virtues for their full expression; for instance, friendliness will require truthfulness, kindness, generosity, and other virtues. Many virtues seem to require or consist in certain desires or emotions, but not always in the same way. Because of these complications, our general account of virtue will be analogous to a definition of "mammal" in a biology book. I can learn the definition of "mammal" and still have lots of unanswered

---

4. MacIntyre points out that Homer did count strength as a virtue. I am describing what most philosophers would say about the virtues, not what every writer has said.

5. See Adams, *Theory of Virtue*, 115–25, for a discussion of psychological research that reputedly undercuts the whole idea of traits of character, including virtues. Without objecting to the empirical evidence gathered by the researchers, Adams explains why their conclusions are overstated. See also my comments on this topic in section 4.1.

6. I discuss the distinction between civility and politeness in Smith, *Virtue of Civility in the Practice of Politics*.

questions about dogs or cats. A general account of virtue merely opens the door to questions about particular virtues.

So far, so good—I have been merely summarizing what many other philosophers have written about the virtues. We come now to a question that divides prominent accounts of virtue. Is the goodness of a virtue *instrumental* or *intrinsic*?

Perhaps the most well-known book in contemporary philosophical ethics is Alasdair MacIntyre's *After Virtue*. In that book MacIntyre argues that Western moral philosophy of the last three hundred years has gone largely astray because it has turned away from important ideas of what MacIntyre calls the "virtue tradition." In telling his history of the virtue tradition, MacIntyre gives a general account of virtue. In chapter 14, "The Nature of the Virtues," MacIntyre offers the following "partial and tentative" definition of a virtue, which is clearly instrumental:

> A virtue is an acquired human quality the possession and exercise of which tends to enable us to achieve those goods which are internal to practices and the lack of which effectively prevents us from achieving any such goods.[7]

This definition makes use of two technical terms, *practice* and *internal goods*, and I will explain them later. For now, it is enough to see that according to MacIntyre's initial definition, the traits we call virtues *are* virtues because they tend to help us achieve something. Other philosophers, such as James Wallace and Philippa Foot, also define virtues instrumentally.[8] According to such views, the presence of virtue in an individual contributes to good outcomes for the individual who has the virtue, or for the society in which she lives, or for both. This raises the further question, what counts as a good outcome for an individual or a society? Many of the philosophers who define virtues instrumentally will say that question is broadly empirical. That is, if we look around at human societies we will see that it is good for human beings to be physically and emotionally well; that it is good for them to have opportunities to develop and use natural gifts; that it is good to engage other people in families, friendships, and other social groups; and so on. Philosophers who give an instrumental definition of virtue would say we don't need to agree on every detail to reach a great deal of agreement on what counts as a good outcome. I think this is largely correct, and at important points the argument of this book will depend on the reader recognizing for himself that certain outcomes are good for human beings.

---

7. MacIntyre, *After Virtue*, 191.
8. Foot, "Virtues and Vices," and Wallace, *Virtues and Vices*.

Some philosophers are attracted to an instrumental definition of virtues precisely because they think this allows them to give a satisfying account of virtue naturalistically. They are rebelling against a long tradition in philosophy, dating back to Plato, that defines virtues by appeal to something nonnatural, that is, the "good" (sometimes capitalized: the Good). Modern naturalistic thinkers are almost always empiricists, with a high regard for science. A nonnatural "good" is scientifically unmeasurable, and to some thinkers it seems to make ethics highly subjective.

In *A Theory of Virtue*, Robert Adams offers a different account of a virtue, in which virtues have *intrinsic* excellence. Adams writes, "I define moral virtue as persisting excellence in being for the good."[9] To explain part of his definition, he says,

> When I speak of "being for the good," *being for* is meant to cover a lot of territory. There are many ways of being for something. They include: loving it, liking it, respecting it, wanting it, wishing for it, appreciating it, thinking highly of it, speaking in favor of it and otherwise intentionally standing for it symbolically, acting to promote or protect it, and being disposed to do such things.[10]

Concerning the idea of "the good," Adams makes use of a concept he developed at some length in his book *Finite and Infinite Goods*.[11] Adams believes there exists one transcendent good, which is God. On Adams' account, every good thing is good by resembling God in some way. There are a great many diverse ways in which good things resemble God: the beauty of art, the sublimity of a waterfall, the rational design of a tool, etc. We rightly judge all these things to be good, because they are in some way like God's beauty, sublimity, rationality, etc. More to the point of this book, moral goods reflect something of God's goodness; human justice, kindness, temperance, and love—all of them imperfect—are good because they reflect God's perfect justice, kindness, temperance, and love.

As I said, a long line of philosophers since Plato has believed in a transcendent good; Adams places himself squarely in that line.[12] However, many philosophers in the Platonic tradition have argued for the *unity* of the virtues, and in practical terms Adams disagrees with them. The Platonic notion here is that since good things in the mundane world are good by

9. Adams, *Theory of Virtue*, 14.

10. Ibid., 15–16.

11. Adams, *Finite and Infinite Goods*.

12 Not all philosophers who believe in a transcendent good are theists. For example, Iris Murdoch was a twentieth-century nontheistic proponent of a transcendent good.

resemblance to one single good, good things are all somehow connected. In particular, the virtues that make for a good character all imply one another—one cannot be truly just without being also honest; one cannot be truly honest without being kind; and so on. Theoretically speaking, Adams agrees that the nature of good things is such that they are all related by resemblance to one transcendent good. But we are finite beings, limited by time and our physical and emotional energies. There are so many good things, and so many aspects in which we can resemble the good, and so many ways of "being for" the good, that in practice, he says, it is often better to speak of "goods" rather than "the good." In the lives of finite human beings, the virtues do not necessarily imply each other; a person may be conscientious, and thus give to charity as a duty, without being generous, a virtue that consists partly in taking pleasure in giving.

According to Adams and others who emphasize the intrinsic value of virtues, moral goodness is worth having for its own sake. Such thinkers readily agree that virtues often do lead to good outcomes for individuals and/or society, but it is important, Adams says, to see that virtues have value even when they lead to no improvement in others' lives or one's own life. I will suggest an illustration.

Imagine an accident at sea. An explosion on a fishing trawler causes the boat to sink in the North Pacific. One member of the crew is left alone, clinging to a partially inflated life raft; the others have all died. Our victim realizes that he will soon succumb to hypothermia; it is beyond reasonable hope for rescue to come in the minutes he has left. Imagine further that in this situation the sailor gives himself to reflecting on good things he has experienced in life: family, health, work, sheer existence. He is grateful for these things; we might even imagine him breathing a prayer of thanks to whatever deity he believes in. Assume that this is not the first time he has thought and felt this way; the man's thankfulness in this situation mirrors a steady habit of his life. Should we say that the man exhibits a virtue?

Those who take a strictly instrumental view of virtues should probably deny that the dying sailor's thankfulness is a real virtue. Perhaps it was a virtue earlier in his life, but not now. It is extremely unlikely that it will lead to any good outcome. No one will ever know about it, and the sailor will soon die.[13] Nevertheless, Adams and others who say that virtues are intrinsically good could readily agree that the sailor exhibits virtue. At the end of his life, he feels appropriate gratitude. (Notice, as I said before, that

---

13. The virtue instrumentalist might say that the sailor's thankfulness is a virtue, because it does lead to a good outcome, namely, his feelings of peace and joy. But this stretches the notion of "leading to" to the breaking point. If there is a last moment in the sailor's life, the gratitude of that moment cannot lead to any good.

some virtues seem to require certain emotions. This is true about gratitude, but we should not generalize to all virtues.) We can imagine that he displays other virtues as well—courage, for example. Now, if we believed the story was actual rather than merely possible, we would admire the sailor for his courage and gratitude. Adams says that our admiration for virtues probably indicates their value better than the results the virtues tend to produce.

> Think of someone very aged and infirm, perhaps unable to move her own wheelchair, and perhaps suffering such memory loss that someone else has to be responsible for many of the decisions in her life . . . if we see notable virtue in her, much of it surely will be in her attitudes, and they may be attitudes to things that she cannot do much about.[14]

I agree with Adams on this point. In the case of the dying sailor and the case of the wheelchair-bound person—and in many other cases in which a moral agent cannot *do* much—we still see character traits that we admire. Therefore, I would contend that virtues are intrinsically good. Further, I agree with Adams' general framework for ethics: that there is a transcendent good, and that good is God. But nothing in the structure of this book or the arguments I will make will depend on these beliefs. Some of the points I make in the book clearly cohere with these beliefs, so if the reader finds my arguments persuasive, she will be more likely to believe in a transcendent good and the intrinsic goodness of virtues. But my arguments and the overall structure of the book make use of MacIntyre's instrumental definition of virtue rather than Adams' notion of being for the good.

My strategy here is to be inclusive. Some readers will agree with Adams (and me) that virtues are intrinsically good and that we should find them admirable even when they lead to no good results. But some will not. If I argued that faith is a virtue on the basis of its intrinsic goodness, I would first have to convert the instrumentalists to something like a Platonic view of the good. No small task! On the other hand, those who believe in the intrinsic goodness of virtues already agree that virtues usually are instrumentally good as well. So I will proceed by arguing that faith is a virtue when viewed instrumentally, and if the argument is sound, it should persuade both groups.

Recall that MacIntyre said that virtues tend to help us achieve the "internal goods" of "practices." MacIntyre defines "practice" this way:

> . . . any coherent and complex form of socially established cooperative human activity through which goods internal to that

---

14. Adams, *Theory of Virtue*, 16.

form of activity are realized in the course of trying to achieve those standards of excellence which are appropriate to, and partially definitive of, that form of activity, with the result that human powers to achieve excellence, and human conceptions of the ends and goods involved, are systematically extended.[15]

Examples will help illustrate MacIntyre's meaning. Throwing a football with skill is not a practice, he says, but the game of football is. Planting turnips is not a practice; farming is. Football and farming are complex social activities. Throwing a ball and planting a row of vegetables are skills of an individual. Practices, since they are social activities, require those who participate in them to communicate with each other—and the standards of excellence appropriate to our practices constitute one of the central topics of our communication. MacIntyre's definition says that the standards of excellence are "partially definitive of" a practice; anyone who wants to participate in a practice needs to learn what it means to do it well. Part of learning how to play football or how to farm is learning what good football or good farming is. Notice that excellence in a practice, such as football, may require excellence in skills, such as throwing the ball, but the reverse is not true. One can throw a football well without being a good football player.

MacIntyre's notion of a "practice" plays a large and organizing role in this book. The main argument, in chapter 3, holds that faith is a virtue because having faith tends to help people achieve the internal goods of three important human practices: scientific research, social/political reform, and parenting. Therefore, I will prepare for that chapter by reflecting in a preliminary way on the idea of a practice.

A great strength of MacIntyre's definition of a practice is that it embeds the concept of a virtue in social living. Philosophers sometimes get so involved in thinking that we forget that virtually all of the best goods of human life are only possible in the context of "socially established cooperative human activity." This truth applies to philosophy itself. Philosophy as an activity can fool us; we are taken in by the image of solitary contemplation. When this happens we believe, like Descartes, that we can start from scratch, avoiding past errors by taking nothing for granted. But the notion is a false one. When I think, I use the language, idioms, and ideas of twenty-first century English (or, with difficulty, the language of some other place and time). I am linguistically embedded in a sociohistorical setting.[16] I *always* take many things for granted. As Ludwig Wittgenstein pointed out, if I tried to think in a completely private language, my symbols/words could have no

---

15. MacIntyre, *After Virtue*, 187.

16. Lakoff and Johnson, *Philosophy in the Flesh* and *Metaphors We Live By*.

grip on the world, or me, since there would be no outside check on their meanings.[17] Philosophy is a MacIntyrean practice, a socially established cooperative human activity; even if philosophers often work on problems alone, we eventually share our thinking with others, and the problems we work on have been shaped by others' ideas.

The social nature of practices gives both objective and recursive qualities to our moral and intellectual lives. Suppose I want to learn a practice, whether it is philosophy, gardening, or architecture. I cannot do just anything at all and call it "architecture." There is an organized human practice called architecture, so if I want to be an architect, I must learn what architecture is from people who participate in it. This provides an objective quality to my intellectual and moral life. In order to move into a practice in any meaningful way, I must learn something of the content of that practice— and this includes learning the standards of excellence in that practice—from those who have been active in the practice before me. I must have enough *humility* to submit to the authority of those who have gone before. At the same time, since a practice is an ongoing human activity, it will necessarily undergo change, because it has to respond to changes in the overall human situation. Somehow the people involved in the practice must come to agree on additions or subtractions from the content of their practice as well as refinements in the standards of excellence of their practice. Who can decide what changes to accept in a practice's standards of excellence? Only those who are already well versed in the practice, that is, those who have (perhaps for a great portion of their lives) been shaped by the active pursuit of excellence in the practice. This is the recursive element in practices; only persons who have already been changed by practices are in a position to change those practices.[18]

Let's go on to the notion of "internal goods." Recall that MacIntyre says that virtues tend to enable people to acquire the internal goods of practices. MacIntyre uses the example of chess to explain the difference between internal and external goods.[19] Imagine an adult inviting a child to learn chess. To motivate the child, the adult promises the child a bit of candy for playing

---

17. Wittgenstein, *Philosophical Investigations*, sections 243–71.

18. One might object that persons outside a practice might try, by force of some kind, to alter the content or standards of a practice. For example, in the Lysenko affair, Stalin's government tried to control the content and standards of excellence in biological research. But the effort failed; over time, the worldwide community of biological researchers rejected Lysenkoism. It's possible, of course, that a government or church could compel everyone involved in a certain practice to conform to alien content or standards of excellence. In MacIntyre's terms, this would be the *corruption* of the practice, or its extinction, if the corruption were total.

19. MacIntyre, *After Virtue*, 188.

and a bit more for winning (promising to play only at a level that will allow the child a chance to win). So the child learns to play and gradually learns to play better. But the adult hopes that the child will learn to play chess not to gain candy but for another good—the good of a well-played chess game. Candy is *external* to chess; the connection between the game and the reward depends on the adult's offer; the child could gain candy in other ways. But the peculiar pleasure of a well-played chess game is only available to people who play chess (or similar games). Perhaps we shouldn't even call this good a "pleasure." But MacIntyre believes, and I think most chess players will agree, that there is an *internal* good produced by chess. (MacIntyre calls it "a certain highly particular kind of analytical skill, strategic imagination, and competitive intensity."[20]) It is internal to chess in two senses: only chess (or some other similar game) will produce it, and only people with experience in chess are competent to judge it.

Notice, says MacIntyre, that so long as the child is motivated only by the candy, she has no reason not to cheat to win (assuming she can get away with it). The more effective her cheating, the more of the external good she gets. But the internal good of chess is completely destroyed by cheating. Thus, external goods often confront practices with the possibility of *corruption*. That is, we can become so enamored with the external goods associated with some practice that we forget the internal goods that make it really worthwhile.

External goods are easy to identify: money (and the things it will buy), prestige, security, etc. We find it harder to give words to internal goods of practices. What should we call the internal goods of architecture? I am an outsider to the practice of architecture, so MacIntyre would say I am incompetent to judge the internal goods of architecture. Architects themselves might find it hard to name the internal goods of their practice. Among them, I suppose, are a measure of difficult problem solving (with related technical details), pleasure in achievement, and satisfaction in meeting human needs. But that's an outsider's guess, and "difficult problem solving combined with pleasure in achievement and satisfaction in meeting human needs" is hardly a convenient label. Nevertheless, I am convinced that architecture has internal goods, and good architects are motivated in their work at least partly by their desire for those internal goods. They're not just in it for the money.

I should be clear: there is nothing wrong with external goods as such. They are real goods. But since they are artificially connected to practices, external goods do not by themselves motivate us toward excellence in our

20. Ibid.

practices. In fact, as in the case of the child chess player and the candy, external goods can motivate us toward vice.

Imagine two partners, an architect and a builder, who think they will not be caught, and who are motivated only by external goods. They ignore the standards of excellence of their practices in order to increase their profits; they construct dwellings just well enough to sell housing to nonexperts. We can imagine them receiving many external goods—community prestige as well as money. Until the earthquake comes, everything looks good. After the earthquake, they blame the government inspector who did not require them to build properly.

Notice that the corruption in this case is really a matter of motivation rather than result. We could imagine the story going slightly differently. Suppose the government inspector forced the externally motivated architect and builder to build according to high standards of excellence. Or suppose the buyers of houses have easy access to reliable third-party evaluators so that market forces motivate the architect and builder to build high-quality buildings. In either case a much better outcome results when the earthquake hits. But it is quite possible that the architect and builder still have lost touch with the internal goods of their practices. If they are motivated only by external goods such as money and prestige and not at all by the internal goods of the practice in which they engage, they are corrupt, in MacIntyrean terms.

As a large-scale social activity, architecture as a whole will not be ruined by one or two—or even one or two thousand—corrupt practitioners. But what would happen if all, or nearly all, people involved in some "socially established cooperative human activity" pursued that activity only for external goods? Suppose that all the architects were indeed only in it for the money. This might not lead to immediate disaster for the public, so long as regulators enforced the standards of excellence that have already been developed. But the internal goods of architecture would disappear. According to MacIntyre, I am not competent to judge what these goods are; nevertheless, I suspect the loss of them would be a very great loss.

If we reflect carefully on the notion of internal goods, we will begin to see that MacIntyre's instrumental definition of a virtue is closer to Adams' intrinsic view than it seemed to be at first. If a practice were completely corrupt, as we were just imagining in the case of architecture, that practice might still produce socially useful results. We imagine all the architects pursuing only money and prestige, but forced by efficient regulators to build excellent buildings anyway. (We are ignoring the real-world problem of bribery; our efficient regulators all exhibit the virtue of honesty.) A corrupt practice, focused exclusively on external goods, might still produce useful things, like excellent buildings, that other people would rightly value. So we don't say the practice is corrupt because it harms other people; it may, but it may not. The practice is corrupt because the practitioners have lost contact with the internal goods of the practice.

It seems, then, that internal goods must be *intrinsically* good; they don't depend on the production (or nonproduction) of useful results. MacIntyre gives us an *instrumental* definition of virtues; they lead to internal goods. But the internal goods themselves seem to be *intrinsically* good—and only those persons who have relevant experience in a practice are competent to judge them.

Naturalistically minded philosophers might be suspicious about this. Internal goods that are supposed to be intrinsically valuable might appear to be just as esoteric and nonnatural as the Platonic "good." Does MacIntyre's instrumental definition of virtue betray naturalism with his concept of internal goods?

Not to worry. We can adopt MacIntyre's account of a virtue and remain thoroughly naturalistic and empirical. If we are curious about the internal goods of some practice (whether they exist and/or what they are like), all we need do is inquire of those people who have achieved competence in that practice. Clearly, there is a "socially established cooperative human activity" that we call playing in an orchestra. As an outsider I can directly observe that this practice enriches the lives of non-players, since I enjoy the music. I also observe that the practice provides the musicians with external goods, including the chance to socialize with other people, the gratitude of listeners, and money (if the orchestra is professional). Beyond all this, I am quite confident that orchestra playing provides the musicians internal goods as well. If I doubted it, I could ask them. Inquiry into the internal goods of practices can be just as much an empirical investigation as social science research on many questions.

Recall that MacIntyre said the definition of a virtue that we have been discussing was "partial and tentative." In chapter 15 of *After Virtue*, "The Virtues, the Unity of a Human Life and the Concept of a Tradition," he expands his initial definition by addressing two further questions.

First: what practices belong to a good life?

Second: what social conditions are needed to support a good life?

In regard to the first question, students have sometimes asked me: what about activities like running a concentration camp or a cocaine cartel? Aren't they examples of "socially established cooperative human activity"? Does this make them "practices"? Could we use MacIntyre's account of a virtue to say there are virtues that tend to produce the "internal goods" of such activities?

Such questions harbor an implicit criticism of MacIntyre's theory, which seems to include too many activities as "practices," and too many human traits as "virtues." The theory needs to somehow draw a line separating unacceptable practices from those that really do contribute to a good life. How does MacIntyre respond to this problem?

We know that different societies have endorsed different virtues. Another strength of MacIntyre's historical account of virtue is that it can explain both the overlap between various lists of virtues and the differences between them. Different societies feature different practices; a practice that is prominent in one society may be unimportant or even nonexistent in another. All societies have the practice of parenting, and they all recognize virtues of good parents. But what is the relationship of good parenting to other practices, such as warfare or religion? Compare parenting in ancient Sparta with parenting in a Pennsylvania Amish village. On MacIntyre's account, since the virtues are embedded in social practices, neither similarities nor differences between Spartan and Amish virtues will surprise us.

But if the differences between various groups' "virtues" don't surprise us, they may worry us. How do we avoid a moral relativism that makes all parenting styles equally good?

In addition to worrying because different societies have endorsed varying visions of the good life, we face another problem. We can observe that human beings have invented a multitude of activities that fit MacIntyre's definition of a practice. A single human being can never be significantly involved in more than a minority of worthwhile practices simply because there are so many of them. Further, the time and commitment of emotional energy required by some practices rule out participation in certain other practices. So how can a person decide wisely which practices she ought to pursue?

Notice that these two questions fuse into a single worry: how do we know which practices really belong in the good life? How can an individual know which practices to incorporate in her life?

MacIntyre says the answer to these worries was traditionally given in the virtue tradition by appeal to the concept of a *telos*. The idea here is one of overall purpose or goal. A human life takes the form of a story, says MacIntyre.[21] We make sense of the events and activities of our lives by explaining to others, and especially to ourselves, how those events and activities relate to the *telos* of human living. But often people do not agree about the purpose of human living. A particular individual may find herself deeply divided, struggling to discern the *telos* of her life. So, both in our lives shared

21. Ibid., 208.

with others and in our individual internal experience, we debate what the purpose of human living is. In a recursive fashion, MacIntyre says that the search for the *telos* of a human life must be part of the *telos* of a human life. And this extends our definition of virtues.

> The virtues therefore are to be understood as those dispositions which will not only sustain practices and enable us to achieve the goods internal to practices, but which will also *sustain us in the relevant kind of quest for the good*, by enabling us to overcome the harms, dangers, temptations and distractions which we encounter, and which will furnish us with increasing self-knowledge and increasing knowledge of the good.[22]

Virtues, then, tend to give us success in searching for the purpose of our lives, as well as in helping us achieve the internal goods of the practices of our lives. The better an individual understands the *telos* of her life, the better she will be able to choose which practices to pursue. On both the personal and social level, we don't need a final answer to every question about the human *telos* (Should I join the orchestra? Is capital punishment permissible?) in order to confidently exclude some options (Should I be a death camp administrator? Does cocaine distribution contribute to a healthy society?).

In regard to the second question (what social conditions are needed to support a good life?), we can observe that no individual's story makes sense without the background of social narrative. Even the hermit monk and the desert island castaway should understand their lives as part of the larger human story. As Aristotle said, a truly solitary life might be the life of a god or a beast, but not a human being.

Paying attention to practices highlights the importance of social background. No one can be an architect or a symphonic oboist in a world without buildings or orchestras. Practices have long histories, involving many people. We know little of most of the people who shaped our current practices—and less about those who will inherit them from us in succeeding generations. A practice evolves over time, so what ties its practitioners together? MacIntyre introduces the notion of a "tradition": "A living tradition then is an historically extended, socially embodied argument, and an argument precisely in part about the goods which constitute that tradition."[23]

---

22. Ibid., 219 (my emphasis). In referring to "the good," MacIntyre acknowledges the Platonic influence on the virtue tradition, which relates the virtues to a nonnatural transcendent good. But MacIntyre's definition is broad enough to include views that locate goods in a purely natural world.

23. Ibid., 222.

Earlier we imagined the practice of architecture corrupted by love of an external good, money. I suggested that even if all the architects were in it for the money, the profession might still produce goods for the public, given honest regulators. But now I want to suggest that architecture, as a living tradition, would be finished. Architecture is not just about designing buildings; architecture is also an ongoing conversation (MacIntyre: "argument") about the goods of architecture.[24] If the architects don't care about the goods of their practice, the conversation/argument will end. MacIntyre thus gives one more refinement of his definition of virtue.

> The virtues find their point and purpose not only in sustaining those relationships necessary if the variety of goods internal to practices are to be achieved and not only in sustaining the form of an individual life in which that individual may seek out his or her good as the good of his or her whole life, but also in *sustaining those traditions which provide both practices and individual lives with their necessary historical context.*[25]

Without living traditions, we would not have practices to join and we would not be able to enjoy the internal goods of practices. Is this a worry? In modern life, we are surrounded by an enormous array of practices, and human creativity continually produces new practices. It seems we have no shortage of living traditions; we seem to have abundant riches in terms of opportunity for good lives. In reply, I would point out that an individual must involve herself in a limited number of practices, and the quality of her life will be bound up with those practices. It will be little consolation to the individual to know that other people are inventing new and wonderful practices if the most important practices of her own life have been corrupted. We all ought to be concerned for the health of the traditions that house the practices of our lives.

Let's return, in a summary illustration, to our example of architecture. Imagine a young college student, we'll call her Sheryl, who dreams of being an architect. She gains admission to a university and enrolls as an architecture major. She begins taking classes, and what she learns overturns some of her preconceptions of the field. As I noted earlier, Sheryl must exhibit some measure of *humility* in order to learn the content and standards of her field. Sheryl finds some of her courses difficult; she must exhibit *perseverance*. During her university years, she learns of some students expelled from the

---

24. Here I apply MacIntyre's notion of "tradition" to a single practice, architecture. I'm not sure MacIntyre would use the term so narrowly, but nothing in my presentation hangs on the difference.

25. MacIntyre, *After Virtue*, 223 (my emphasis).

architecture program for cheating on tests; certainly to be a good architecture student, Sheryl must be *honest*. We could go on. These are the virtues Sheryl needs, simply considering her as an individual aiming to participate in a practice.

Long before Sheryl began her studies, architecture existed. Architects both agreed and disagreed about new ideas within architecture involving materials, aims, methods, styles, and other matters. As a beginner, Sheryl learns what others have said and done. But as she graduates from university and builds her career as an architect, Sheryl begins to contribute to the ongoing conversation inside architecture. She adopts some ideas. She rejects others. Perhaps she innovates and shares her new idea with the discipline. In all this we can see that Sheryl and other architects again need *honesty*; deception will undermine their conversation. (Notice that Sheryl's university education, by punishing cheating, tried to train her in the virtues necessary for the discipline. Of course, university officials may have done this unwittingly.) In order to propose new ideas, Sheryl and other architects may need *courage*. In judging which new ideas to incorporate into their practice, all architects need *practical wisdom*. These are virtues Sheryl and the other architects need, considering architecture as a practice and a tradition.

Sheryl engages in many practices besides architecture. Maybe she takes part in a book discussion group. She may marry, become a parent, and join a parent-teacher association. Perhaps she takes up gardening, playing violin in a community orchestra, teaching in Hebrew school, or running marathons. As I stressed earlier, the variety of practices available in modern life—and the internal goods achieved through them—is vast. In all this complexity, how can Sheryl make sense of her life? She will need *wisdom* to find practices that both fit together and fit her. She will need a kind of *self-control*, to be able to say no to intriguing opportunities that really don't fit her life. Excellence in most things takes time and repeated efforts to achieve, so Sheryl will again need *perseverance*. Some of the best goods we know come to us as internal goods of intimate relationships; as a daughter, friend, lover, or parent, Sheryl will need *faithfulness*.[26] These are among the virtues Sheryl will need as she struggles to unify her life, that is, to make her life *a good life*, rather than a series of disconnected happenings.[27]

I will now recapitulate our general account of virtues.

26. I promised earlier that I would not use faith as an example in this chapter. The reader should infer that though faithfulness may be related to faith, I regard them as different virtues. Rather than *faithfulness*, I might use *fidelity*.

27. I do not imply that unity is sufficient to produce a good life, but a reasonable degree of unity is necessary for a good life. Without some unifying narrative, a human life will be experienced as "one damn thing after another."

1. Virtues are characteristics of human beings.

2. Virtues are acquired; acquisition usually takes time and effort.

3. Virtues are enduring tendencies, not isolated incidences or ironclad laws of behavior.

4. Particular virtues will have differing psychological structures, involving emotions, desires, and intentions in varying ways.

5. Virtues are intrinsically valuable. (Though I think this is true, it will not figure in the argument of this book.)

6. Virtues are instrumentally valuable. They help us achieve good outcomes in at least three different ways: *a*) virtues tend to help us achieve the internal goods of practices; *b*) virtues tend to help individuals as they seek for unity in their lives, a unity that gives meaning to the practices they engage in; and *c*) virtues tend to sustain practices and traditions over time, giving background and context to individuals' pursuit of good lives.

Alert readers will probably realize that this first chapter has contributed nothing new to the philosophical discussion of virtues. Practically every idea in the chapter has been harvested from the prior work of Robert Adams and Alasdair MacIntyre. Obviously, that does not make these philosophers responsible if I have misinterpreted their work. But the dependency of this book on others' work nicely illustrates how philosophy is a MacIntyrean practice.

Human beings are social creatures. We are dependent on each other in so many ways that we rarely notice them. Without doing anything to deserve the many gifts that have been bestowed on me, I am given life, language, books, relationships, mentors, moral examples, and moral opportunities—along with nonmoral goods like beauty in the world around me, physical vigor, abilities to sense the world, mental capacities, and so on. Some of these are the gifts of God or nature, and some of them come through people. I have many reasons to be grateful; in particular, I have reason to be grateful to Adams and MacIntyre.

It need not be said, but I will say it anyway: anyone who reads this book must occupy a place much like mine. You exist, you have been taught language, you have sufficient mental capacities to read and follow philosophical argument, and so on. It seems that *gratitude* is an appropriate virtue for author and reader alike.

2

A Definition of Faith

The main argument of the book: faith helps us achieve the internal goods of research science, social/political reform, and parenting, and these practices are very important to good living; therefore faith is an important virtue for good living. Chapter 1 defined "virtue" as it functions in this argument; the next step is to define "faith."

Easier said than done. Asking, "What is faith?" is much like asking, "What is a game?"

The philosopher Ludwig Wittgenstein wrote that questions such as "What is _____?" often lead us astray.[1] We think that there must be some thing that corresponds to our word. The word may be *meaning*, or *time*, or *faith*, or something else entirely. But there may not be any one *thing* named by that particular word. Wittgenstein famously offered the example of games. If we pay attention, he wrote, we will see that there is no single common feature to games, but instead there are many "family resemblances" among games. We discover this, not by meditating on the word *game*, but by *looking*. That is, we pay attention to the way people actually use the word. I propose we do this with *faith*.

People use *faith* in a variety of ways. I will list eight different meanings people assign to *faith*. The list is *not* exhaustive; people undoubtedly use *faith* in more ways than these. But the list demonstrates, I think, that there is no single meaning of *faith*, and no single common feature to these usages. The eighth definition is my own proposal. I do not say it is the true or best

---

1. Wittgenstein, *Philosophical Investigations*, sections 65 and 66, and *Preliminary Studies*, 1.

understanding of the term; there is no single true or best understanding of the term. I offer my definition of faith because it serves the purposes of the argument of the book and because it captures an important way many people use the word.

Because people use *faith* to mean different things, they often talk past each other when they discuss faith. I say faith is a virtue, but someone else says it is a vice. If we recognize that we may mean different things by *faith*, we're much more likely to understand each other.

It's possible that at some point readers of this chapter will think, "Well, that's not what I mean by *faith*." That's all right. I am going to offer *a* definition of faith, not *the* definition of faith. Perhaps when you use the word you are talking about something other than what I call faith, and perhaps the thing you mean by *faith* is something worthy of a separate discussion. The argument of this book only asks that you consider my contention that the human characteristic that I will call faith is a vital part of good living.

Having acknowledged that people mean different things by *faith*, I do think that the understanding of faith developed in this chapter (which I will call faith$_{(8)}$) tracks important features of the way both religious and nonreligious people speak of faith. I hope that the definition of faith I propose will be neutral in this sense: both those philosophers who think faith is a virtue and those who think it is a vice will agree that the definition describes an important concept that can rightfully be called faith.

After I survey eight versions of faith, I will refine faith$_{(8)}$ by using some features of the earlier versions to enrich the concept in faith$_{(8)}$. In section 2.2 I will discuss the affective and volitional component of faith, and in section 2.3 I will defend my contention that faith must have a cognitive component.

2.1 VARIETIES OF "FAITH"

On to the list!

Faith$_{(1)}$: "Faith is believing what you know ain't so." Samuel Clemens (Mark Twain) put this memorable phrase in the mouth of one of his characters, Pudd'nhead Wilson. It's a joke, of course, but the joke has a certain bite because we recognize some truth in it. That is, some people seem to affirm, by "faith," things that they know, or ought to know, are false. Charles Dodgson (Lewis Carroll) offered a similar joke, in *Through the Looking Glass*. Alice says to the White Queen: "There's no use in trying. One *can't* believe impossible things." The White Queen answers: "I daresay you haven't had much practice. When I was your age, I always did it for half-an-hour a day. Why, sometimes I've believed as many as six impossible things before breakfast."[2]

I imagine that Mark Twain and Lewis Carroll aimed their ridicule at real targets. That is, they knew people who used "faith" like Pudd'nhead Wilson. Some people really have thought that faith means believing impossible things or believing something one knows to be false.

Having admitted that some people speak this way, we need to see that they shouldn't. People who think faith involves believing things known to be false are wrong, first of all, about belief. If I *believe* a thing, I must *think that it is true.* This is what philosophers call an "analytic truth." One need not interview bachelors to confirm that they are unmarried men; we know this simply by knowing what *bachelor* means. In a similar way, the concept of belief includes the concept of regarding as true. To say, "I believe this, but it's not true" is as unintelligible as saying, "I am a bachelor, and that woman is my wife."

If faith$_{(1)}$ were the only version of faith in our language, I would be the first to agree that faith is an intellectual vice. My contention that faith is a virtue clearly does not extend to all uses of "faith."

Faith$_{(2)}$: faith is believing without doubts. The notion here is that faith and doubt are inversely proportional to each other. On this view, the degree that a person has doubt about something is the degree of her disbelief in it. Some Christians interpret certain biblical passages as supporting this view; for instance, Jesus chastised Peter when the disciple failed to walk on water: "You of little faith, why did you doubt?" (Matt 14:31 NIV). Whether or not this passage really means that doubt and faith are antithetical, it is certain that some people read it that way.

If people have imbibed the notion that faith is opposed to doubt, and if they think that faith is a good thing, it is easy for them to develop an *unwillingness to consider evidence* against their faith. Such reluctance to consider counterevidence comes in degrees. Some people may be merely hesitant to consider counterevidence, while others may energetically avoid it. In extreme cases, some people deny that there is any *possible* counterevidence to their beliefs. Peter Boghossian, a philosopher at Portland State University, identifies such unfalsifiable beliefs as "cognitive sickness."[3]

Since the reluctance to consider counterevidence comes in degrees, we should be slow to make a blanket judgment about all cases of faith$_{(2)}$. A completely unfalsifiable belief—that is, a belief against which the believer

2. Carroll, *Alice's Adventures in Wonderland & Through the Looking Glass*, 174.

3. Boghossian, "Faith, Belief and Hope." It is possible that professor Boghossian would include other "faiths" from my list as cognitive sicknesses, but he would certainly include unfalsifiable beliefs.

will allow no *possible* evidence of any kind—is a bad belief. Boghossian is right about that. But a person may be slow to consider counterevidence for a belief for good, practical reasons. It might be true that the extreme case is a "cognitive sickness" while the mild case is a cognitive virtue. For example, teammates in basketball generally believe that each member of the team is striving for team goals (primarily, winning). Suppose it occurs to player L (for loyal) that one of her teammates, S (for selfish), might be pursuing individual glory rather than team success. In most cases, good teammates simply dismiss this worry out of hand. Loyal player L doesn't bother to weigh evidence for or against the belief, because wasting mental effort on such questions distracts from the immediate task of playing well together as a team. In this case, player L's mild reluctance to consider counterevidence is actually a good thing. But suppose overwhelming evidence comes to light that player S is not only pursuing her own interests over the team's goals, but she also has been deliberately "throwing" games to pay off debts to a bookmaker. Player S is both self-serving and a cheater. Now suppose loyal L's faith in selfish S remains unshaken; player L will not allow *anything* to weaken her belief. When the mild reluctance has become a complete refusal to consider counterevidence it has become a bad thing, a "cognitive sickness."

Faith$_{(3)}$: faith is a special way of acquiring and maintaining beliefs. Sometimes one can meet people who say, "I choose to believe . . ." This understanding of faith brings *will* onto the scene. Faith$_{(3)}$ does not go to the extreme of faith$_{(1)}$, since faith$_{(3)}$ does not mean belief in things known to be false or logically impossible. Faith$_{(3)}$ restricts the operation of the will to a certain class of beliefs.

Philosophers have long debated the propriety of allowing will any role in belief formation. W. K. Clifford said that it is wrong for anyone, anywhere, at any time to believe anything on insufficient evidence. Since only evidence counts, there is no room in the belief business for wishful thinking, hoping, or faith. William James replied that there are some forced-choice situations in which we must either believe something or else not believe it, that in some of these situations purely "intellectual grounds" will not decide the issue, and that sometimes these forced choices are important enough that it is morally acceptable to *choose* to believe. That is, James implied, there are some situations in which beliefs might be rightly based on something other than evidence. Lest we think this debate is a mere artifact of the 1890s, when Clifford and James wrote, in 2005 Simon Blackburn began his book *Truth: A Guide* by rehearsing the Clifford and James arguments (and siding emphatically with Clifford).[4] Faith is clearly a bad thing, says Blackburn. "Intellectual grounds" *will* decide most issues, Blackburn says, and when they won't, we can simply refrain from believing. "Refusing to believe is not a kind of faith."[5] For Blackburn, there are no forced-choice situations such as James imagined.

The debate between Clifford and James focused mostly on religious faith, with Clifford arguing that religious beliefs, if not founded on good evidence, are evil, and James claiming that persons may properly believe in God by choice. Blackburn sides with Clifford, but says that the debate about religious beliefs is only an illustration. Faith cannot be admitted as a shortcut around evidence in any case. What we want to be true is simply irrelevant to what is true, Blackburn insists.

Notice that faith$_{(2)}$ and faith$_{(3)}$ are not co-extensive. A person *may* hold both positions—that faith is inversely proportional to doubt *and* that faith is a special route to achieving beliefs. But nothing about faith$_{(2)}$ requires faith$_{(3)}$, or *vice versa*. Analogous to what Wittgenstein said about games, we see family resemblances, not essential features.

Faith$_{(4)}$: faith is not a special way of acquiring beliefs, but is a commitment of one's life toward one's beliefs. Faith$_{(4)}$ is well expressed by Arthur Holmes:

> Faith is neither a way of knowing nor a source of knowledge. Faith is rather an openness and wholehearted response to God's self-revelation. It does not preclude thinking either about what we believe or about what we are unsure of, nor does it make it unnecessary to search for truth or to examine evidence and arguments.[6]

C. S. Lewis's view paralleled Holmes's:

> Now Faith, in the sense in which I am here using the word, is the art of holding on to things your reason has once accepted, in spite of your changing moods. For moods will change, whatever view your reason takes. I know that by experience. Now that I am a Christian I do have moods in which the whole thing looks very improbable; but when I was an atheist I had moods in which Christianity looked terribly probable.[7]

---

4. Blackburn, *Truth*, 3–13.

5. Ibid., 13.

6. Holmes, *Idea of a Christian College*, 18.

7. Lewis, *Mere Christianity*, 123.

Faith$_{(4)}$ is clearly incompatible with faith$_{(3)}$. Holmes explicitly and Lewis implicitly deny that faith is a special way of acquiring beliefs. Now, some Christians think of faith along the lines of faith$_{(3)}$, and in these excerpts Holmes and Lewis are writing explicitly as Christians. The obvious conclusion to be drawn is that Christians disagree about what "faith" is; at the least, they do not completely agree about it. I'm confident the same is true for Muslims and Jews. This realization underscores the importance of paying attention to various uses of "faith." It's not just that believers and unbelievers speak past each other when they debate faith; coreligionists sometimes speak past each other as well.

For Holmes and Lewis, faith concerns what one *does* about one's beliefs. Here we can benefit from a distinction made by medieval theologians. There are two parts to faith: *fides* (the thing believed) and *fiducia* (the attitude taken toward the thing believed). For example, Christianity requires that one believe (*fides*) that God was in Christ reconciling the world to Himself, but the Christian also commits herself (*fiducia*) to this belief. The *fiducia* aspect of faith includes affect and volition, feelings and actions. Holmes and Lewis insist on the *fiducia* element of faith; for them, it is the defining aspect of faith. For both, acquiring beliefs is a matter of reason and evidence; faith is what you do with beliefs once you've got them.

Faith$_{(5)}$: faith is a gift of God, given that a person might believe things necessary for salvation. Here, faith is explicitly understood as religious faith, as faith in God and in whatever truths are necessary for salvation. The philosopher Alvin Plantinga is a representative of this view, which he finds in Thomas Aquinas and John Calvin. Plantinga seems to think of the gift of faith as a natural capacity "built in" to human nature; he uses Calvin's phrase *sensus divinitatis* for this semi-perceptual cognitive power. The idea is that in many ordinary circumstances of life, human beings "sense" God. They then believe in God, not on the basis of an argument, but basically.[8] Consider an analogy. Suppose someone asks you what you had for breakfast, and you answer, "The quiche looked runny, so I had the omelet." Your belief that you chose the omelet is not based on evidence or reasoning; you simply remember what you had for breakfast. This is a "basic" belief. In appropriate circumstances you just find yourself believing something. In a similar way, Plantinga argued, persons may, in certain circumstances, simply find themselves believing things like "God made all this beauty," or "God is displeased with my shabby behavior." In such circumstances, the *sensus divinitatis* simply informs us.

8. Plantinga, "Reason and Belief in God."

Another version of faith$_{(5)}$ would see the gift of faith as an event in a person's life. On this view, God directly gives a person belief in things crucial to salvation.[9] Philosopher Robert T. Herbert quotes a character in Graham Greene's *The End of the Affair*: "I've caught belief like a disease," and "I fell into belief like I fell into love." Herbert's position is that coming to believe is, in at least some cases, neither reasonable nor unreasonable. It is simply something that happens to a person. The occasion of the gift might be any sort of event in the person's life: a vision of beauty, a rational argument, an experience of suffering, and so on.

Aquinas famously affirmed that some items of dogma could be demonstrated by argument; for instance, that God exists can be shown by right reason. However, some people may not be able to understand the arguments that demonstrate these truths. Such simple folk believe by faith—a gift of God—things that learned people can know through demonstration. But Aquinas did not think that all truths of Christianity could be demonstrated by reason. For these items of dogma (e.g., that God exists as a Trinity), all the faithful are dependent on revelation. In any case, we need the gift of faith (as *fiducia*) to properly align our lives with the teachings of the church.

Faith$_{(6)}$: two kinds of faith should be distinguished; *thin* faith is not the same thing as *thick* faith. Jay Wood, a philosopher at Wheaton College, defines thin faith as trust in our basic epistemic faculties.[10] Thick faith, on the other hand, is belief in some comprehensive doctrine, such as some particular religion or ideology.

It's important to take notice of the difference between thin faith and thick faith, not least because it shows the fallacy of a certain argument often used against agnosticism.

Let me illustrate the notion of thin faith. 1) I must *trust* my senses to navigate through a day. 2) I have to *believe* that the words and phrases I use in thinking today are part of the same language I used yesterday. 3) I may doubt this or that memory belief, but the only way to correct memory beliefs is to check them against other beliefs, including memory beliefs, that I am *not doubting*. 4) If I don't *depend* on fundamental logical moves such as *modus ponens*, I can't reason at all. Sensory beliefs, memory beliefs, and dependence on logical inferences are examples of thin faith, and Wood is certainly right that we must have thin faith if we are to engage in intellectual work.

Sometimes religious people will argue this way: "Everyone needs to have some kind of faith, so really it is only a question of which faith one will

9. Herbert, "Is Coming to Believe in God Reasonable or Unreasonable?"
10. Wood, "Faith's Intellectual Rewards."

adopt. Disbelief in God is just as much a matter of faith as belief in God." Stated just that baldly, the argument is ambiguous and fallacious. Professor Wood's distinction between thin faith and thick faith helps us see why. It is true that everyone must have thin faith, but it is not true that everyone must have thick faith. Agnostics are able to engage in intellectual work—precisely because they do trust their basic epistemic faculties—while at the same time not subscribing to thick religious or ideological faith.

Atheists, unlike agnostics, seem to take a position on a thick faith question. Perhaps atheists think, on the basis of sense perception, memory, or logic, that the existence of God can be disproved. If that were true, their disbelief in God would be knowledge and not faith. But if there is no such proof, their disbelief in God really is just as much a matter of faith as is religious persons' belief in God. In contrast, the agnostic's *fiducia* faith in her epistemic faculties does not commit her to any religious position.

Faith$_{(7)}$: faith is the trust we place in subsidiary knowledge while we strive for focal knowledge; at the same time, faith is trust that the focal knowledge we strive for is attainable. The terms "subsidiary knowledge" and "focal knowledge" are derived from the work of Michael Polanyi.[11]

Polanyi's epistemology represents a radical break from most Western epistemology, from Plato to Plantinga.[12] To appreciate the depth of Polanyi's rebellion, we need to consider (briefly) what the Western tradition has said.

Philosophers have assumed throughout our history that we must first understand what knowledge is before we can figure out how to get it. What is knowledge? What is the difference between mere opinion and knowledge? These and like questions have dominated more than two millennia of epistemology.

Knowledge is *justified true belief*, someone might say, a view often attributed to Plato. That is, for something to be knowledge, you have to believe it, and it has to be true, and you must have good reasons for believing it.[13] But what reasons count as good reasons for believing something? What *justifies* holding a belief?

Thomas Aquinas illustrates a historically important answer: foundationalism. Foundationalists hold that most of our beliefs should be derivable from basic beliefs. Beliefs are justified if they are *basic* beliefs or derived

---

11. In this section I depend on the development of Polanyi's insights in Meek, *Loving to Know*.

12. Meek, "Michael Polanyi and Alvin Plantinga."

13. Contemporary epistemologists would not affirm a JTB theory of knowledge without modifying it to account for Gettier problems. See Gettier, "Is Justified True Belief Knowledge?"

from basic beliefs. For "classical" foundationalists like Aquinas, the basic beliefs are either self-evident truths or truths that are evident to the senses.[14]

René Descartes and David Hume together undermined our confidence in truths evident to the senses. First, Descartes set the standard for knowledge at *undoubtability*. He worried about the possibility that he might be dreaming rather than perceiving the real world. In the most extreme case, Descartes thought, if it is possible that an evil demon is deceiving me, I can't rely on my perceptions to deliver real knowledge. So the mark of true knowledge is that it is impossible to be wrong: undoubtability. Philosophers like John Locke cheerfully accepted the undoubtability standard, thinking that they could prove the reliability of the senses (and the existence of God, and lots of other things). But David Hume came along and pointed out that all of our perceptual beliefs rely on our prior belief that a real world *causes* our perceptions—and our belief in causation is itself not a self-evident belief, nor a perceptual belief, nor derivable from either self-evident beliefs or perceptual beliefs. Hume concluded that belief in causation is akin to superstition. And if we don't have good reason to believe in causation, we have no good reason to trust our senses. Hume recognized that we are overwhelmingly predisposed to believe in causation and the deliverances of our senses, but that only means that we should admit that we live in a world beyond our capacity to really know.[15]

Hume's skeptical conclusion was something of a scandal in its own time (Kant certainly thought so), and it has motivated much epistemology in the last three centuries. It is embarrassing that in the era of modern science some of the best epistemologists say we don't really know anything. Don't we live in the era of the knowledge explosion? And yet epistemology in the last century has not escaped the shadow of Hume. It seems crazy to say we don't know things; we're learning all the time. But epistemological theories seem to multiply like Tribbles, mostly in the vain attempt to find a watertight definition of knowledge.

Now we can appreciate the radical nature of Michael Polanyi's epistemology. Polanyi was a Hungarian medical doctor and physical chemist, but his interests extended to economics, politics, and philosophy. Polanyi thought that the epistemology of the mid-twentieth century made no sense of the way scientists actually work. He started, not with the question, "What is knowledge?" but with, "How do we know?" Scientists do gain knowledge—how do they do it? Polanyi's epistemology rests on an insightful

14. Plantinga, "Reason and Belief in God." Plantinga seems to be a foundationalist, but not a classical foundationalist; he would include belief in God among basic beliefs.

15. Hume, *Treatise of Human Nature*, part 3, section 14.

exploration of the process of knowledge acquisition. He steadfastly resists getting sidetracked by the desire for a definition of knowledge.

What happens when we come to know? Think of knowing as a *process of discovery*. How does the process work? Polanyi thought that his greatest discovery was the "structure of tacit knowing." We move from "tacit" knowledge or awareness to "focal" knowledge or awareness. Consider learning to read.[16] When we were children we learned the shapes of letters and the sounds they represent. We learned to blend the sounds together to make words, and we spoke the words in order to grasp their sense. In Polanyi's terms, we directed our *focal awareness* to letters, sounds, and words. But later, after having learned to read, our attention shifts. Suppose you are reading a loan contract for a house. Now, your focal awareness is on the *contract*, an abstract entity, rather than on the paper and ink. You are thinking of the responsibilities and obligations you will take on if you sign the contract. Notice: while you are reading the contract, you rely on—Polanyi would say you *indwell*—the words and sentences on the paper. You have *subsidiary* awareness of the letters and words; you are probably not conscious of them. Your conscious attention is on the matter of focal awareness, the contract.

Esther Meek says the process of coming to know displays faith in two ways. First, we *trust* subsidiary things while we strive to understand the focal things. Second, the whole process is motivated and sustained by belief that truth is *there to be found*; the focal understanding we desire can be achieved.[17]

Polanyi pointed out that our subsidiary awareness is *tacit* rather than explicit. A well-trained doctor, when using a probe to explore some organ inside a patient, relies not on sight (since the organ is inside the patient's body) but on the *feel* of the probe in her hand. She gains insight into the state of the organ by *relying on* a kind of knowledge that she probably could not express verbally. Another illustration: think of keeping your balance while riding a bicycle. Many parts of your body may be involved in this complex behavior—your arms, legs, inner ear (sense of balance), eyes, your butt on the seat, a feeling in your gut. All are included in subsidiary awareness, but rarely are you consciously aware of any of them. In fact, says Polanyi, our subsidiary knowledge is indeterminate; it is impossible to say precisely all that goes into it. We are *embodied* knowers. We also exhibit faith, says Meek, in our pursuit of focal knowledge. We trust that there is something "out there," something to be known, and we can gain some measure of understanding of it. A measure of understanding—but not complete

16. Meek, *Loving to Know*, 70.
17. Ibid., 94, 170.

comprehension! Polanyi and Meek say the mark of the real is that the new insight opens up new questions.[18] The process of coming to know moves from one kind of indeterminacy (not-completely-specifiable subsidiary awareness) to a different kind of indeterminacy (a focal insight that opens up unpredicted further avenues of exploration).

Faith$_{(7)}$ has affinities with "thin" faith when it is our reliance on subsidiary awareness we have in mind. But faith$_{(7)}$ also coheres with other versions of faith in this list, at least in the sense that it does not contradict them. Once again, we find overlaps and family resemblances among our concepts, not a clean taxonomy.

Meek claims: "All knowing has as its structure and dynamic the subsidiary-focal integrative feat as identified by Polanyi."[19] If she is right, faith$_{(7)}$ is as ubiquitous as "thin" faith. We need it in order to know anything. Does faith$_{(7)}$ go beyond "thin" faith? Does our reliance on subsidiary awareness go beyond basic epistemic faculties? It seems the answer is yes. Only a trained physician can use the probe to extend her knowledge in the right way. For the untrained person, the probe is just an awkward piece of machinery.

On Meek's view, faith$_{(7)}$, since it is crucial to the whole process of coming to know, would seem to be worthy of my focus in this book. Nevertheless, my focus is somewhere else. Faith$_{(7)}$ is bound up with Polanyian epistemology. This book doesn't focus on epistemology, but on morality. I am writing about a virtue the possession of which helps one achieve the goods of important human practices: scientific research, social and political reform, and parenting. I will return to faith$_{(7)}$ in chapter 5, when I discuss the case of Henrietta Leavitt, but for most of this book our attention will be on faith$_{(8)}$.

Faith$_{(8)}$: faith is believing and being for things that are not known and are not believed by people who are epistemologically close to us. Two parts of this definition need immediate comment. First, faith$_{(8)}$ involves believing things not known. A few paragraphs back, I noted that modern epistemologists have worked very hard in the futile (so far) effort to find a definition of knowledge they can all affirm. My definition of faith$_{(8)}$ does not depend on settling this debate. It doesn't matter which theory of knowledge you adopt; faith$_{(8)}$ only applies to things you do not know—given your theory. We all admit that there are many things we believe that we do not know, so there is a very wide field of applicability for faith$_{(8)}$.

Second, faith$_{(8)}$ involves believing things that other people—people who are epistemologically close to us—do not believe.

18. Ibid., 75.
19. Ibid., 67.

Many people today live at what might be called great epistemic distance from us. This distance was as great, if not greater, in the past, when people lived in cultures with significantly different plausibility structures than ours. (Certainly there are contemporary cultures of which the same may be said.) For example, a medieval European might have believed that the blood of noble persons is purer than the blood of commoners. This belief is so distant from a modern, scientific, liberal mindset that we can understand it only with effort. (What did "blood" or "purity" mean in the medieval context? At a minimum, "blood" meant more than the fluid in one's veins and "purity" meant more than something chemical.) The belief is so implausible to us that we do not consider evidence for or against it. So far as we consider the matter at all, we reject the medieval belief as a matter of course. Our un-thinking rejection of the medieval belief is a kind of faith. (But not faith$_{(8)}$! It is somewhat like faith$_{(7)}$.) It is a faith that lies in our shared life. We *live* this way—a form of life that combines beliefs about the physiology of blood, the role of DNA in human reproduction, and the equal political worth of every person. Of course, we could stop to think carefully about the medieval belief, and we would discover that we have strong evidence for our contrary beliefs about blood and DNA; to that extent our rejection of the medieval belief in noble blood is based on evidence. But what is the evidence for our belief in the equal political worth of every person? Thomas Jefferson thought it was self-evident—which is an admission that he knew of no evi-dence for it. And yet it is clear that many people in many times and places have not thought the equal political worth of all persons is self-evident; in fact, the Nazis thought it obviously false. Belief in the equal political worth of all persons is a kind of faith. It is somewhat like Jay Wood's thin faith, in that it is unquestioned bedrock of the way we (some of us, anyway) live. But belief in the equal political worth of persons doesn't really fit the thin faith category, since the Nazis proved one can do intellectual work while denying it. As I said earlier, this list—faiths 1 through 8—is *not* complete.

The point of the illustration is that some people live or lived at great epistemic distance from us. The distance between such widely divergent belief systems serves to insulate us from them. For instance, I believe that airliners fly because the air passing over their specially designed curved wings creates lift. This is a rational belief for me, not because I am an expert in aircraft design, but because I remember learning about this in school. A great many of our rational beliefs are like that—we learn them from relevant authorities who, if called upon, can explain the evidence for the beliefs. Now, I think it is safe to say that no medieval Europeans (except da Vinci?) had any beliefs about the shape of airplane wings and lift. Perhaps it is not quite right to say they didn't believe what I believe, since the idea never occurred to them. It would seem strange to say the medieval Europeans had a "faith" concerning the shape of airplane wings if they had no beliefs about the matter. Therefore, when I suggest that faith involves believing things other people don't believe, in the usual case I mean people whose epistemic world is relatively close to mine.

Experientially, it is not the beliefs of "distant" persons that trouble us. I can read a book and learn that samurai culture included certain beliefs. It is an intellectual exercise only; I am not tempted to adopt samurai beliefs. In contrast, suppose I read an editorial in a newspaper or on a website that supports capital punishment, while I myself oppose capital punishment. The writer gives reasons for the policy he supports, and in the process he expresses a number of beliefs. Now I am challenged. Here is someone who inhabits an epistemic world very close to mine, and yet we do not agree. Why does the writer believe the things he does? Should I, perhaps, adopt his beliefs?

I suggest that faith—faith as a virtue, a component of good living— most often occurs in such settings. Faith involves believing things that are not believed by people who are epistemologically close to me. In fact, they are people for whom I have intellectual respect: I regard them as well in- formed and rational.[20] Yet they believe differently than I do. My knowledge that a well-informed and rational person does not believe as I do almost always gives me grounds for doubting whether what I believe is true. If nothing else, I can think of that person as giving well-informed and rational testimony against my belief. If I nevertheless believe that it is true, my be- lieving is *usually* faith.[21] In chapter 3 I will argue that such believing is part of good living.

If a philosopher I respect says there is no God, I have reason to doubt there is a God. If I continue to believe in God, it will be because I think that if *all* the relevant evidence were on the table it would demonstrate the existence of God. But of course, in regard to belief in God—and in regard

---

20. Someone might object that if a well-informed and rational person believes a thing then all well-informed and rational people ought to believe it. This mistakes "well-informed and rational" for "omniscient and perfectly wise." I will return to the question of what we ought to believe in chapter 3.

21. Something like the following could happen. I could recognize that someone else, for whom I have intellectual respect, believes p while I believe ~p. This causes me to reexamine my position. Upon reexamination, I find that my belief seems very well supported by evidence; I am convinced it is a rational belief. It doesn't seem right to me to call my belief faith, since it is in accord with reason. And yet, the other person, whom I respect, does not agree. I am at a loss as to what to think about the other person's belief. And he may be just as dismayed by my belief. Neither of us regards his position as "faith," since he thinks it is in accord with reason.

to *many* important other questions in life—we live our lives without all the relevant evidence.

This is where faith$_{(8)}$ lives. We are fully aware of people whom we respect—intelligent, well-informed, and well-intentioned people—who do not believe some of the things we believe. Nevertheless, we continue to believe those things. I contend that faith$_{(8)}$ occurs commonly. It is a faith that coexists with doubt in the typical case. Note the explicit contrast with faith$_{(2)}$, which pictures faith and doubt as inversely proportional.

Faith$_{(8)}$ includes both *fides* and *fiducia*. It is not enough to believe something is true; one must also be *for* it. This is such an important point that I will devote section 2.2 to it.

I claim—and this is the most important assertion of this section—that faith$_{(8)}$ describes the attitude many people hold toward many beliefs; faith$_{(8)}$ has many instances in real life. In chapter 3 I will argue that faith$_{(8)}$ is a virtue.

2.2 BEING FOR: THE AFFECTIVE AND VOLITIONAL COMPONENTS OF FAITH

In this section, I adopt, nearly wholesale, Robert Adams' position that faith includes affective and volitional components. In chapter 16, "Moral Faith," from *Finite and Infinite Goods* (1999), Adams says that merely believing a thing is not sufficient for faith: "To have faith is always to be *for* what one has faith in."[22] In 2006 he published *A Theory of Virtue*, in which he explained his broad notion of *being for* something, in a passage I cited in chapter 1.

> There are many ways of being for something. They include: loving it, liking it, respecting it, wanting it, wishing for it, appreciating it, thinking highly of it, speaking in favor of it and otherwise intentionally standing for it symbolically, acting to promote or protect it, and being disposed to do such things.[23]

Suppose some person, Elaine, believes that a hurricane will strike her coastal county within forty-eight hours. Elaine's belief is not irrational; after all, hurricanes do occur, her county does border the ocean, and it is hurricane season. Let us assume that her belief is not shared by all of Elaine's neighbors. Perhaps the weather service has predicted that the hurricane might come ashore somewhere else or not strike land at all. The mere fact that reasonable people around her do not believe that the hurricane will

22. Adams, *Finite and Infinite Goods*, 384.
23. Adams, *Theory of Virtue*, 15–16.

strike their county ought to give Elaine some cause to doubt her belief. Nevertheless, Elaine does believe that the hurricane will strike and will devastate the county.

We are not now focusing on whether Elaine's belief is well grounded, rational, or right. As we will see in the next chapter, some philosophers have said that Elaine ought to strictly regulate her degree of belief to the amount of evidence she has for the belief. We will leave that question for chapter 3. The point I am focusing on now is this: Elaine's belief about the hurricane is not faith, because she is not *for* it. In fact, Elaine feels a mixture of despair and dread whenever she thinks about the hurricane. She is *against* the hurricane, though she finds it very hard to express her opposition to it. Taking precautions before the hurricane strikes and cooperating in reconstruction efforts afterward seem terribly inadequate as means of expressing her opposition to the hurricane. Such practical actions may help limit or alleviate the bad effects of the storm, but in regard to the storm itself they are symbolic actions.[24] We might say that Elaine's attitude toward the hurricane is that it *ought not to be.*[25]

This feature of faith, that it includes our affections and volitions, is a long-standing part of religious tradition. "You believe that there is one God. Good! Even the demons believe that—and shudder" (James 2:19 NIV). The demons, according to this text, are *against* God in much the same way as Elaine is against the hurricane. The apostle takes it for granted that the demons do not have real faith. If faith is to be a virtue, it must include more than intellectual assent, says James: "faith without deeds is dead" (James 2:17, 26 NIV).

Adams' notion of *being for* something includes feelings, attitudes, desires, and hopes in regard to it, as well as symbolic actions favoring it and actions that promote or protect it. Thus he includes both our affections and our volitions in the notion of *being for*. That sounds right to me, and it steers us away from unnecessary complications.

We might be tempted to ask precisely which affections or volitions are required to transform belief into faith. Suppose a college soccer player believes his team will win the conference championship. He rejoices at the thought; he is excited by the prospect of a championship; and he confidently predicts to his friends that the team will win the conference. Nevertheless, he exhibits poor practice habits: he arrives late, doesn't work hard, and

24. See Adams, *Finite and Infinite Goods*, 214–49, for a discussion of symbols and the ways we use them to express ourselves as being for the good (or against the bad).

25. See Neiman, *Evil in Modern Thought*, 5. Neiman identifies as basic to our judgment that something is evil the thought: *this ought not to have happened; it ought not to be.*

distracts his teammates with irrelevant conversation. My goal is to imagine a case in which the player's affections seem right but his volitions are wrong. Should we say he has faith that his team will win the championship? "Faith without deeds is dead," says the apostle, and we can imagine the player's coach would agree. In this case it seems that belief plus affect is not enough; real faith should show itself in the player's behavior. But not all examples are like the soccer player. Imagine a fan of the same college soccer team who believes, not that the team will win the conference, but that the coach is an excellent coach: knowledgable, hardworking, dedicated, and so on. His belief gives the fan confidence that the coach is doing the right thing when, for example, he hears other people criticize the coach's strategy or substitutions during a game. He rejoices at successes by the team, and he thinks the coach deserves partial credit for those successes. It is completely possible that the fan's belief and confidence in the coach produce no observable actions on the part of the fan. Perhaps he doesn't even verbally defend the coach when he hears others criticize him. The fan simply attends games and feels a sense of satisfaction and approval in watching good coaching. I think we should say that the fan has faith in the coach; in this case belief plus affect seems enough.

I may not have imagined or described these examples just right. Someone might say that the soccer player does have faith that his team will win the conference, but that he lacks other virtues, such as self-control and the determination to work hard. I think the point of the examples still stands, however: the proper affect/volition that combines with belief to constitute faith may vary in different cases.

What about the person whose religious faith is combined with anger at God? Suppose a longtime religious believer experiences great evil in the world—his family is destroyed as a result of ethnic cleansing, or he is betrayed by a trusted friend, or he is diagnosed with a terminal and painful disease. Understandably, many persons of faith have reported feeling great anger at God in these sorts of situations. Should we say that these people are against God? Surely being angry at something can be one way of being against it. Should we therefore say that these people do not have faith in God, at least while their anger lasts?

In most cases, I think such a person exemplifies what Adams calls "clinging to faith."[26] The believer believes that God exists and is kind and just; yet, in his suffering, he does not experience God's kindness or justice. The anger the believer feels toward God arises from this contradiction. We might say the believer is *for* the God he believes in but *against* the God

---

26. Adams, *Finite and Infinite Goods*, 386.

he experiences. Eventually, believers resolve this tension, either by rationalizing their experience in a way that allows them to incorporate it into their beliefs about God, by abandoning belief in God, or by gradually losing their anger. (Theoretically, one could retain one's belief in God and settle into a determined opposition to God, à la James's devils.[27] But I don't know of any such accounts.) The faithful are sometimes angry at God, but such anger does not last forever; if it did, they would cease to be faithful.

I agree with Adams that faith involves *being for* the thing believed, but that leaves open the *way* in which one is for the thing believed. Most of the time, we might guess, faith will involve both affect (feelings, desires, etc.) and volition (decisions and actions). But we don't need to try to make a rule that tells us how much of either is required—cases will differ.

A more important question is not how much affect or volition is required for faith, but whether affect and volition together simply *are* faith. Does faith really need belief? We turn to that question next.

2.3 WHY FAITH MUST INCLUDE BELIEF

As we will see in chapter 3, some philosophers have thought that all our believing ought to be strictly governed by evidence. They would say that faith, if it involves believing something more strongly than the evidence indicates, is a bad thing. At the same time, such thinkers might agree that a good life sometimes includes feelings and decisions that involve us in risk. So they might say that "faith" could be a good thing (in some circumstances), but only as a combination of affect and volition. We don't need to *believe* beyond the evidence, they would say, in order to *feel* and *act* beyond the evidence.

Such objectors might offer an example along these lines. Suppose there is discord in a marriage over money. Husband and wife argue over money, and each occasionally undermines the family budget by making large unilateral spending decisions. The situation builds to a crisis. The couple sees a counselor, who tries to help them understand why they use purchases to "one-up" each other. Both husband and wife seem to understand the situation better, and they promise to each other to change their financial practices.

Now, our objecting philosophers will say, the husband and wife may well act on "faith"—understood as each *being for* the healing of the marriage. That is, each one *wants* the marriage to succeed; each one *loves* the other; each one *decides* to change. The husband and wife make a *commitment* to a common project. But in none of this do they *believe* anything to

27. See James 2:19.

any degree beyond what the evidence supports. They both know that the other has promised to change, and they both can estimate how likely it is that the other will change. At first they might struggle with a lot of doubt, but as time goes on and each one sticks to the new financial discipline, both wife and husband come to believe more firmly in the other's repentance.

If "faith" is to be a virtue, the objectors could argue, isn't that the way we should understand it? Conceived this way, faith is a combination of affect and volition, but it doesn't require belief.[28] Consistent with what we said in chapter 1, the objectors could point out that this "faith" interweaves with other virtues, such as love and tenacity. But beliefs should always be governed by evidence.

I would counter that faith does require belief, even in the marriage case just described. Notice, though, that I don't need to show that faith includes belief in every case. The burden of proof goes the other way. The objector wants to define faith as only affect and/or volition, not as belief that goes beyond the evidence. If faith, conceived as something that contributes to good living, requires belief in some cases but not others, that is still enough to show that good living sometimes requires a faith with a cognitive component.

I will say two things to support the idea that faith requires belief in at least some cases. First, I will relate an example to illustrate a comment by Adams. Suppose that "John" and "Henry" correspond frequently by email. They live on different continents and have never seen one another. Henry has a position of midlevel authority in the government of a small developing country. He has steadfastly refused to participate in bribery and other corruptions that infest the ministry where he works, and this has drawn him into increasing conflict with ambitious coworkers. Some of these people threaten Henry. They demand that he collaborate with some of their dishonest schemes, or else they will destroy his career with false accusations.

Henry asks John for his advice. John quickly learns that Henry has good reason to believe that his enemies have the power to carry through on their threats. The ministry and the local courts are fairly rife with corruption. The whole episode causes John to feel thankful for the comparatively honest courts and civil service in his own country, but he realizes that he cannot apply his expectations of government in his country to government in Henry's country. Now, how should John advise Henry? Should he encourage him to persist in his rejection of bribery and his pursuit of efficient, honest public service? Or should he tell Henry to act in ways that Henry has already described as corrupt?

28. Louis Pojman takes this position. See Pojman, "Faith, Hope and Doubt."

Adams says:

> Morality requires that we encourage each other to live morally. But how could we do that in good conscience if we thought living morally would be bad for the other person? Are we to encourage others to act morally so that we, or the less scrupulous, may take advantage of them, or so that we may all lose out together? Those are not morally attractive propositions; but if, on the other hand, we cease to encourage each other to act morally, we have abandoned morality as a social enterprise. So it seems that if we do not believe that living morally is at least normally good for a person, there will be a conflict in the very soul of our morality that threatens to tear it apart.[29]

Does John believe that moral living is good for Henry? Perhaps it would be a good thing for Henry if he were to succeed in leading an anti-corruption campaign. But John has no expectation that such a campaign would succeed. If Henry persists in his honesty, John expects that it will cost Henry his career and possibly much more.

We can easily imagine, or find in history books, cases that parallel the John and Henry case. Should the "Johns" in these stories advise the "Henrys" to risk great loss (martyrdom, in many actual cases) for what is morally right? Adams' point is this: morality requires that we do so, and yet morality requires that we not do so, unless we *believe* that acting morally is at least normally good for the moral person. It is not enough that we *wish* or *desire* that moral living be good for our friends; we need to actually *think* that it is good for them. And yet it seems easy to find rational and well-informed people who deny that such moral living really is good for the moral person. Friedrich Nietzsche comes to mind. Nietzsche famously scorned the "slave morality" of inferior people that threatened the full living of better people. He emphatically denied that "noble" people should limit their lives according to slave morality.[30]

The objector may try to argue this way: "We only need to believe that acting morally is good for the person to the extent that evidence seems to suggest that it really will be good for the person. Our beliefs can be regulated by evidence, while our moral faith consists in our emotions and decisions." But this will not work. Adams is right that morality requires us (at least sometimes) to encourage our friends to act morally even when the cost to them is high, and we cannot in good conscience do so if we think that it would be bad for them, all things considered.

---

29. Adams, *Finite and Infinite Goods*, 377.
30. Nietzsche, *Genealogy of Morals*, section 10.

Let's move away now from the example. The second thing I want to say to defend the cognitive component of faith is simply an observation about human psychology. To wit: for human beings, believing, desiring, and willing are interrelated. For more than one hundred years, since Freud at least, psychologists have been saying that our believings, desirings, and willings are interrelated subconsciously; we are never fully aware of how they influence each other.

Now if this picture of the human mind is at all accurate—that there is a subconscious mind and that our beliefs, desires, and decisions interact with each other—it seems highly unlikely that the virtue of faith could exist purely as a combination of desire and decision. The cognitive component of faith will get dragged in because of its influence on affect and volition. To illustrate the point, let us imagine another player on the college soccer team, this time one who has excellent practice habits. This player *wants* his team to win the conference championship and he *behaves* in ways that help make him a better player and his team a better team. But since he believes that several other teams in the conference are superior to his, he rejects out of hand the notion that his team will win the conference. He simply doesn't believe it. And for that reason, it's wrong to say he has faith that the team will win the conference. He has the right affect and volition, but without the appropriate belief, he doesn't have that faith.

It will be instructive to pursue the example a bit further. If the player doesn't believe the team will win the conference, why does he persist in his excellent practice habits? What sustains him in the face of difficulty, discomfort, disappointment, and lazy teammates? Most likely, the player believes in something—not that the team will win the conference, but that something valuable can be gained by striving for excellence in soccer. The player does have a faith of some sort, and it involves belief, even if the player could not clearly express that belief.

2.4 SUMMARY DEFINITION

Faith$_{(8)}$: believing and being for something that is doubtful (in the normal case, something not believed by persons for whom one has intellectual respect). Believing something involves thinking that it is true. "Being for" something involves affect and volition.

2.5 ADDENDUM: REGARDING "PROPOSITIONS"

Some readers, particularly those trained in philosophy, will have noticed that thus far I have avoided using the word *proposition*, except when quoting someone else. I have employed *thing* or *something*, as in the statement "Faith is believing something." Some may think I have perversely used a vague word when a more precise word is available. So I should explain.

First of all, there is a difference between the words we use to describe something and the thing itself. A Christian has faith in God. She uses many words (e.g., "I believe in God the Father Almighty, maker of heaven and earth," etc.) to describe God. Her faith is not in those words, but in the reality to which they point. It is quite proper, even necessary, for Christians to use propositions to describe God. How else could they do many of the things essential to their religion, such as public worship, religious instruction of children, and so on? Nevertheless, the Christian may come to be dissatisfied with some proposition or group of propositions she has previously employed. (Maybe for the first time in her life she has encountered horrific evil; her previous attempts at theodicy now sound empty and weak to her.) The Christian may well come to deny some of the propositions she formerly used to describe her belief in God, and yet rightly insist that she still believes in God. In fact, she may say that her belief in God—the real God, not just the object of her creed—is stronger than ever.

It should be clear that nothing hangs on the religious nature of the previous example. A scientist may have faith in a research program and yet be willing to modify many of the auxiliary hypotheses that compose the program. A parent may have faith in something for which she finds no adequate proposition at all. Much like the second soccer player, she believes that there is something good, something worthwhile, to be achieved by means of the struggle in which she is engaged, but she may not be able tell you what that good is.

Second, I have been wary of saying that faith means believing a proposition because the phrase sounded, at least to my ear, exclusively cognitive. I very much want to guard against the idea that faith is entirely or mostly belief *that*. Faith must include *being for* the thing believed. The cognitive component is necessary, as I argued in section 2.3, but so are the affective and volitional components.

These two worries compound each other. "The hurricane will strike our county" is simply a proposition. Elaine believes it. But when we say that Elaine is against the hurricane, it is the reality we describe with those words that she detests, not a mere statement.

Having offered these words of explanation, I will now abandon my resistance to using *proposition*. I only beg the reader to remember that if I speak of faith in a proposition, I mean faith in the thing the proposition is used to express, and being for that thing.

3

~~~

Why Faith Is a Virtue

This book holds as its main thesis that faith$_{(8)}$ is a virtue. A virtue, as explained in chapter 1, is an acquired characteristic of human beings that tends to help them achieve the internal goods of practices, to direct and aid them in the search for unity in their lives, and to sustain practices and traditions. Faith$_{(8)}$, as explained in chapter 2, consists in believing and being for something doubtful, something that is not believed by people one respects intellectually. This chapter will argue that faith$_{(8)}$ can be a virtue, because it helps us achieve the internal goods of three very important practices: scientific research, social/political reform, and parenting.

A note on terminology: from here on, when I use the word *faith* with no subscript, I mean faith$_{(8)}$. I will continue using subscripts when I refer to the other versions of faith discussed in chapter 2.

When arguing for some position, it is often helpful to know what one is arguing against. Therefore, before I examine the role of faith in the three practices just mentioned, I will cite a few philosophers who would say that faith should be listed among the vices rather than the virtues. The key question is whether and in what way it could be virtuous or praiseworthy to believe something doubtful.

3.1 THE ETHICS OF BELIEF

We begin with a familiar fable (famous at least among philosophers) given, with its equally famous moral, by W. K. Clifford in the 1890s. He tells of a shipowner who suffered doubts about his aging vessel. The ship was old and perhaps not too well built. It had weathered hard storms. Maybe the owner ought to pay for a complete refitting. But he talked himself into believing the ship was seaworthy. After all, the ship had crossed the ocean many times before. Clifford emphasized that the shipowner sincerely believed the ship would sail safely. Nevertheless, the ship sank, killing all aboard. The moral of the story? The shipowner had *believed* immorally. If we suppose the ship had the good luck to reach port safely, that would not change the moral status of the ship owner's believing. Clifford wrote:

> The sincerity of his conviction can in no wise help him, because *he had no right to believe on such evidence as was before him.* He had acquired his belief not by honestly earning it in patient investigation, but by stifling his doubts.[1]

And:

> To sum up: it is wrong always, everywhere, and for anyone, to believe anything upon insufficient evidence.[2]

Many other philosophers have agreed with Clifford, including Bertrand Russell, Brand Blanshard, and more recently, Simon Blackburn.[3] It is important to note the strong tone of moral censure in these authors. For instance, Blackburn:

> And of course, Clifford is right. Someone sitting on a completely unreasonable belief is sitting on a time bomb. The apparently harmless, idiosyncratic belief of the Catholic Church that one thing may have the substance of another, although it displays absolutely none of its empirical qualities, prepares people for the view that some people are agents of Satan in disguise, which in turn makes it reasonable to destroy them.[4]

I would point out, as an aside, that though Blackburn says the Catholic belief in transubstantiation (which I do not share) predisposes people to destroy others, he does not give any evidence for the causal relationship he claims. It is probably true that some people have indeed moved from this particular religious belief to condoning murder. But some people have also moved from secular beliefs, such as belief in the Marxist labor theory of value, to condoning murder. Both trains of reasoning are fallacious. How does one get from "one substance can have the attributes of another" to

1. Clifford, "Ethics of Belief," 1. The emphasis is Clifford's.
2. Ibid., 5.
3. See Russell, "Why I Am Not a Christian," and Blackburn, *Truth*.
4. Blackburn, *Truth*, 5.

"some people ought to be destroyed"? How does one get from "the value of a thing is the labor required to make the thing" to "capitalists ought to be destroyed"? In each case the conclusion simply does not follow from the premise, unless the premises of both arguments are augmented with other propositions, including moral propositions. Yet I would guess that in the twentieth century alone, the latter secular fallacy was associated with the murder of more people than in the entire history of Catholicism.

Be that as it may, the question Clifford and Blackburn put before us is this: isn't faith actually a vice? To have faith means believing beyond the evidence, and that is always wrong. Never believe anything on insufficient evidence: this is the doctrine of *evidentialism*. We ought to notice a few features of evidentialism before considering whether or not it is true.[5]

First of all, evidentialism endorses the common sense notion of degrees of belief. Most of us find, when we consider our beliefs, that we believe some things more firmly than others. I believe that orange juice is a good source of vitamin C. I also believe that supplying my body with vitamin C will help me avoid catching a cold. However, I believe the first proposition far more strongly than the second. I've read conflicting reports about vitamin C as a cold preventative in the popular press; I suspect that newspaper and television health reports drastically oversimplify the actual research results; and I have never taken the time to read any real scientific reports. So my confidence in vitamin C as a cold preventative is not very high—certainly not high when compared to my confidence that I take in vitamin C every time I drink orange juice.

According to evidentialism, my beliefs about orange juice and vitamin C are perfectly good beliefs, if I have conformed the strength of my beliefs to the evidence. The evidentialist rule (never believe anything on insufficient evidence) implies a corollary: never believe more strongly than the evidence warrants. If the evidence for a certain proposition is slightly stronger than the evidence against it, evidentialism permits me to believe it—but only to a slight degree. My weak belief in the cold preventative powers of vitamin C could fall into this category. Going further, the evidentialists would say my belief in vitamin C as a cold preventative should be even weaker if I have not put much effort into investigating the claim. Their doctrine holds that not only must I regulate the strength of my belief by judging the evidence I know (for and against), but I also must temper my belief by estimating whether I have done a good job in discovering evidence (for and against).

5. Some readers will be familiar with Alvin Plantinga's critique of evidentialism in "Reason and Belief in God." The preliminary criticism of evidentialism given in this section is based loosely on Plantinga's work.

To paraphrase Clifford: if a person won't make the effort to investigate a matter, he is wrong to believe anything about the matter.

Second, it should be emphasized that evidentialism is a *moral* doctrine. It gives us a rule that we are supposed to obey, to wit: never believe anything on insufficient evidence. This is a prohibition, along the lines of "Do not commit murder." Now, a single moral prohibition does not constitute a moral system or theory. Consider the prohibition of murder, for example. Every important moral theory—social contract theory, utilitarianism, Kantianism, divine command theory, and others—endorses this moral rule. This is hardly surprising, since we wouldn't take seriously any moral theory that didn't condemn murder. The various theories of ethics agree that murder is wrong, but they differ in their explanations of *why* murder is wrong. The social contract philosopher says that murder violates a rule rational beings would agree to for their mutual benefit; the utilitarian says it detracts from overall human happiness; the Kantian says murder fails as a universal rule of conduct; the divine command theorist says it disobeys God's command; and so on. In a similar fashion, evidentialists might say that their rule could be justified by a variety of ethical theories.

Notice that we should not abandon our belief that murder is wrong, even if we come to believe that social contract or utilitarian ethical theories don't work. Suppose someone thought that *no* ethical theory currently on offer was satisfactory. He could still rightly affirm that murder is wrong, though he would be frustrated by his inability to explain why it is wrong. In a similar way, the evidentialists could say their doctrine does not stand or fall with any particular ethical theory or even with all of the theories currently propounded by moral philosophers. If you find some evidentialist defending his doctrine on utilitarian grounds (as Clifford and Blackburn seem to do) and you think utilitarianism fails as a moral theory, you should not for that reason condemn the evidentialist rule.

Evidentialists might say that, considered as a stand-alone command, the evidentialist prohibition (never believe anything on insufficient evidence) ought to strike us as obviously true, just as the murder prohibition is obviously true. One of the ways we test moral theories is to see if they give adequate explanation for such truisms.[6] We are immediately suspicious of a philosophical theory, such as emotivism or cultural relativism,

---

6. Philosophers call moral truisms "pretheoretical beliefs." We do not expect a moral theory to confirm *all* our pretheoretical beliefs; most of us are willing to be convinced that some of our moral beliefs are mistaken, and a good ethical theory might help convince us. But we are very unlikely to believe a moral theory that overturns most or all of our pretheoretical beliefs.

which undermines our confidence in moral truisms.[7] Evidentialists could conclude that we ought to be as suspicious of a moral theory that has no place for a prohibition against believing on insufficient evidence as we are of theories that have no place for a prohibition against murder.

While I do not think the evidentialist rule is right, I think there is a kernel of truth in evidentialism, because often it is important to search out evidence and to conform the strength of our beliefs to the evidence that we find. If we transformed evidentialism from a hard-and-fast rule into a piece of exception-admitting advice, there would be no problem with it: "Usually it is wise to conform one's beliefs and the strength of one's beliefs to the evidence one finds for those beliefs." But the evidentialists will have none of that. They want a universal rule: "It is wrong always, everywhere, and for anyone, to believe anything upon insufficient evidence."

The third thing to notice about evidentialism is that it cannot possibly work as a universal rule. We can suppose that an evidentialist *believes* the following proposition:

> (E) It is wrong always, everywhere, and for anyone, to believe anything upon insufficient evidence.

Now, what is the evidence to support proposition E? If there weren't sufficient evidence to support proposition E, then it would be wrong to believe proposition E, on its own terms.[8] Without evidence in its favor, proposition E becomes self-defeating. Further, the evidence in support of proposition E would have to be particularly strong evidence to justify such a sweeping prohibition. One would think that if the evidentialist were aware

7. Emotivism is the doctrine that moral propositions merely express the speaker's feelings; they cannot describe states of affairs. According to emotivism, "murder is wrong" really means that "I don't like murder and I don't want you to like it either." Cultural relativism is the doctrine that all moral judgments are "true" or "false" according to the standard beliefs of some cultural group. According to cultural relativism, "murder is wrong" means only that within some cultural group murder is regarded as wrong.

Emotivism and cultural relativism both imply that our ordinary understanding of the moral truism is mistaken. Notice I say this makes us suspicious of these theories. Suspicion alone is not reason enough to reject a theory. Philosophers have produced strong arguments undermining both emotivism and cultural relativism; for example, see Rachels, *Elements of Moral Philosophy*, 12–38.

8. Some readers may be confused or bothered by the whole idea of "evidence" for a moral proposition like proposition E. They are accustomed to thinking of moral beliefs as wholly different from factual beliefs, so that evidence doesn't really apply to moral beliefs. I think this is a lingering effect of the positivistic era in twentieth-century philosophy. Unfortunately, this footnote could grow into its own chapter if I were to relate the rise and fall of positivism and explain why its overly narrow conception of evidence ought to be ignored. Perhaps it is enough to note that neither the evidentialists nor I are at all bothered by the notion of evidence supporting a moral belief.

of counterevidence that speaks against the truth of proposition E, he should at the least temper the strength of his belief in proposition E.

Most evidentialists *are* aware of such counterevidence. There are, after all, things we believe without any evidence at all. Remember Jay Wood's distinction between "thin" faith and "thick" faith from chapter 2. A thick faith$_{(6)}$ is a comprehensive collection of beliefs, such as Judaism (a religion) or Marxism (an ideology). Thin faith$_{(6)}$ is the trust we place in our basic epistemic faculties, such as memory, logical intuition, and sense perception. Let's concentrate for the moment on sensory beliefs.

As an empiricist, David Hume insisted that all our knowledge of the world around us had to come via sensory experience. But he saw clearly that mere experience tells us nothing about the world around us, unless we make certain assumptions. For instance, we assume that the world causes our experience. We have to distinguish between two sorts of beliefs. If I believe (1) *I am seeing a cat,* I must also believe (2) *there is some feature of the world (the cat) that is causing me to have the visual experience of seeing a cat.* If I came to disbelieve (2), I would have to change (1) into something else: (1A) *it seems to me that I am seeing a cat.* Proposition 1A leaves open the possibility that what I am seeing is caused by something other than a cat.

We clearly do believe (at least in most cases) that the world around us causes our sensory experiences. We think we see real cats and sidewalks. Now if someone (a Hollywood movie producer, for example) suggests to us that most of our experiences are not actually caused by the world but are fed to us by a controlling computer (we being merely bodies housed in pods), we dismiss the possibility without a care (though we may still enjoy the movie). The evidentialist, when he is careless, will say the evidence amply supports our belief that the world causes our perceptions of it. Doesn't all our experience speak in favor of it? What counts against it, except the fantasies of the moviemaker?

This response misses the force of Humean skepticism. Hume pointed out that our "superstition" about causation is what allows us to believe that the future will be relevantly like the past. If someone suggests that beginning tomorrow the daisies will start singing in Latin, we won't believe it. Nothing in our experience lends any support to such a bizarre idea. But Hume asks: what evidence do we have that supports our belief that the future will be like the past? Exactly zero. We have no evidence at all about our future experiences unless we believe there is a world that causes our perceptions of it and that the world is relevantly stable—one that we can understand. Someone might object that we have always expected the future to be like the past, and our expectations have been sufficiently rewarded. Hume might grant that this is true about our *past* experiences and still insist: *tomorrow* is a completely unknown quantity; nothing about the past is in any way relevant to the future unless both are features of a relatively stable world that causes our experiences.

Ludwig Wittgenstein said that the beliefs that "stand fast" are like the foundations of a house—but the foundations are "carried" by the whole house.[9] In another metaphor, he likened them to an axis:

> I do not explicitly learn the propositions that stand fast for me. I can discover them subsequently like the axis around which a body rotates. This axis is not fixed in the sense that anything holds it fast, but the movement around it determines its immobility.[10]

The proper response to the Humean skeptic, who wants to say that we do not really know that the world causes our experiences of the world (and, therefore, what we perceive as the world might be a chimera), is to say: well, we live this way. Belief in causation is simply part of our form of life. We do not know how to imagine living without this belief. My initial response to the "hard" evidentialist, who wants to say we must conform *all* our beliefs to the evidence, is similar. Some of our beliefs lie deeper in our way of life than any evidence we could give for them. We simply live this way.

A more careful evidentialist—not W. K. Clifford, but perhaps Simon Blackburn or Peter Boghossian—will admit that there are certain background beliefs or fundamental assumptions that we do not believe on the basis of evidence. The evidentialist prohibition is not supposed to apply to those beliefs. After all, background beliefs like our belief in causation really are shared by virtually all of us—and I have already said that faith involves believing doubtful things, that is (in the typical case) propositions that other people do not believe.

The more careful evidentialist has moved away from the hard evidentialism of proposition E, which was:

> (E) It is wrong always, everywhere, and for anyone, to believe anything upon insufficient evidence.

But the more careful evidentialist still wants a rule, a prohibition, against wrong believing. Essential to the new rule, however it is formulated, would be a distinction between certain fundamental beliefs (such as belief in causation), which can be believed rightly without evidence, and all other

---

9. Wittgenstein, *On Certainty*, section 248.
10. Ibid., section 152.

beliefs, which should only be believed on the basis of evidence. We might express this softer evidentialism this way:

> (E1) It is wrong always, everywhere, and for anyone, to believe anything, *except fundamental background beliefs like belief in causation*, upon insufficient evidence.

It is at this point that Alvin Plantinga claimed that *belief in God* could be rightly included among the "properly basic" beliefs—beliefs that can be rightly held without any evidence at all.[11] As you might expect, the careful evidentialists are not happy with this move. If someone can include as controversial a belief as belief in God among the "properly basic" beliefs, it seems that anything goes. Plantinga was aware of this objection (the "Great Pumpkin" objection). He denied that his position entailed that "anything goes" when it comes to beliefs. And he agreed that there are moral duties in the business of believing.[12] But Plantinga did not offer a guideline or set of rules by which one could tell whether her "basic beliefs" were "proper" or not.

I am not going to explore Plantinga's contention that belief in God is "properly basic" at this time. I am going to delay discussion of religious faith, whether and in what way it may be a virtue, until chapter 8. What I have said already about faith suggests a better way for the careful evidentialist to express his rule.

> (E2) It is wrong always, everywhere, and for anyone, to believe things *that are not believed by persons for whom one has intellectual respect* upon insufficient evidence.

I believe proposition E2 gets at what the careful evidentialist wants to say, because it rules out Plantinga's contention that belief in God can be part of the background beliefs. It would be better, of course, for the careful evidentialists to express their own position. Notice that proposition E2 takes direct aim at the kind of believing I identified as faith$_{(8)}$ in chapter 2. There I said that in the typical case faith is believing and being for things that are not believed by persons for whom one has intellectual respect. E2 clearly says that faith so defined is always morally wrong. Thus, if the careful evidentialist is right, faith is a vice, not a virtue.

Earlier I said that if evidentialism were reduced to a piece of good advice, we would have no problem. Let's make the comparison explicit, by comparing E2, above, with what I will call "Advisory Evidentialism":

11. See Plantinga, "Reason and Belief in God."

12. Ibid., 149–52 and 115.

(AE) Usually it is wise to conform one's beliefs and the strength
of one's beliefs to the evidence one finds for those beliefs.

I think E2 is false, while AE is true. If Advisory Evidentialism (AE) is
true we will discover many cases that seem to support Careful Evidentialism (E2). Any case in which someone believes something in accord with
evidence and which we would judge to be wise believing—that is, a case
that supports Advisory Evidentialism—will also be a case that supports
Careful Evidentialism. What we need to find are counterexamples to E2,
cases in which the following conditions are all present. First, someone
believes something that is not believed by people for whom she has intellectual respect. (Call this person the believer.) Second, the believer believes
the controversial proposition more strongly than her evidence seems to
warrant. Third, there is nothing morally wrong with the believer's belief.
Fourth, in accordance with the overall argument of this book, having the
belief should tend to help the believer achieve the internal goods of some
important practice(s).

Evidentialists must not at this point simply define away counterexamples. What I mean is this: A careful evidentialist, for whom E2 seems
just obviously true, will be tempted to say, "Look, in the case under consideration, so-and-so believed more strongly than the evidence warranted.
Therefore, it *had* to be an immoral belief." Obviously, this begs the question. The right procedure is to look at actual cases—particular occasions
of believing beyond the evidence—and ask ourselves whether the beliefs in
question were immoral. Did the beliefs in question help the believer achieve
the internal goods of important practices? If we find cases that fit the four
conditions in the prior paragraph, those cases count as evidence against E2.

3.2 FAITH AS A VIRTUE IN SCIENTIFIC RESEARCH

I will begin my search for examples by considering research science. The
reader will remember that we are considering science as a MacIntyrean
practice. We are thinking of science as a "coherent and complex form of socially established cooperative human activity through which goods internal
to that form of activity are realized." Faith will be a virtue in the practice of
science if having faith tends to help scientists achieve the internal goods
of science. So we start with that question: what are the internal goods of
scientific research? What goods does science make available to us that are
not obtainable in any other way?

Science aims to produce knowledge in the form of better understanding of the natural world. Notice the importance of *understanding*. The

knowledge that science pursues must not be confused with mere enumeration of facts. To see this point clearly, imagine some would-be scientist standing on his lawn on a summer's day. The would-be scientist begins his research career by recording the facts he observes. He could start by counting the blades of grass under his feet. He could list the insects he finds in his lawn. He could note which blades of grass a particular insect touches as it hops or wiggles across the lawn. And so on. Given a finite human life span, such a "scientist" could devote his entire career to enumerating observations from a single day in the yard. There is an indefinite and for all practical purposes infinite number of factual observations that could be made by any simple observer. Obviously, real science does not pursue that kind of knowledge.

To gain *understanding*, scientists propose *theories*. Scientific theories do lots of things: they categorize facts, they define entities (observable and unobservable), they make causal explanations, and they provide causal predictions. We can say that all scientific theories aim at understanding, but we need to beware of making that too simple. Scientists propose theories as answers to questions, and since people have varied questions about the world around them, scientific theories vary in their explanatory aims. A taxonomy that categorizes certain creatures (whales and manatees) together while distinguishing them from others (salmon and sharks) is just as much a scientific theory as one that enables us to predict solar eclipses or another that describes the behavior of unobservable entities such as neutrons. Scientists also offer theories to answer questions in the social sciences, and such theories may define entities like "market demand" and make predictions or explanations using such concepts.

So the internal good of science (at least, one of the internal goods of science) is the production of understanding of the world around us, and this is accomplished through the creation of good theories. But what counts as a good theory? That's a complicated business, and much philosophical work has been given to delineating the features that make some theories better than others. Six features have been proposed: 1. First and foremost, a scientific theory must answer at least some of the questions scientists have in their area of study. 2. Good theories ought to account for empirical observations that scientists have already made. 3. Good theories ought to direct scientists toward further work, both by suggesting ways to test the theory by new observations (predictiveness) and by opening up new lines of inquiry (productiveness). 4. Good theories ought to be comprehensive, tying together previously unrelated data. 5. Good theories ought to be simple, in the sense of explaining lots of data by means of a few powerful concepts. 6. And good theories ought to be beautiful.

As you might expect, philosophers of science debate the nature and relative importance of each of these characteristics of good theories. For instance, how important is it that a theory adequately account for the empirical data so far accumulated in a discipline? On first blush, one might think a good theory ought to cover all the data, but in practice this turns out not to be the case. A theory can succeed on other criteria—in terms of predictiveness, productiveness, comprehensiveness, or beauty—even though it explains only some of the empirical observations made so far. Scientific theories are accepted or rejected *over time by a diffuse but socially cooperative group of people*, that is, scientists working in the discipline. In other words, research science is a MacIntyrean practice. Each scientist in the field weighs the criteria for theory choice in his or her own way and the scientists working in a discipline interact with each other in multiple ways. The features of a good theory listed in the previous paragraph are those often mentioned by scientists and philosophers of science, but precisely because science is a "socially established cooperative human activity," it is impossible to construct a precise recipe for evaluating a good theory.

What role does faith play here? One way to answer this question is to note the role of background assumptions in experiments. In the hypothetico-deductive model of scientific practice, the scientist first proposes a hypothesis, which answers some question(s) scientists have had about their field. The hypothesis ought to account for at least some of the data scientists have already gathered. Next, the scientist deduces from the hypothesis some prediction for future observations. Ideally, this prediction ought to be novel, that is, something no one has yet observed. Armed with a novel prediction, scientists can then devise a "crucial experiment" to see whether the predicted observations pan out. Sometimes it takes a great deal of ingenuity and resources to conduct such experiments.

We can schematize the testing of a theory in this way:

$$T \rightarrow P \rightarrow O$$

The theory (T) leads to the prediction (P), which is then tested by observation (O). What happens when the predicted observation doesn't pan out? According to one theory in philosophy of science, called falsificationism, this is actually what makes scientific progress possible. When the result of the experiment is not what was predicted (we would symbolize this as ~O), we have refuted, or at least have definite evidence against, the theory. At least, this is what the falsificationists, such as Karl Popper, claimed.

But there are problems with falsificationism. First, it doesn't describe the actual practice of scientists very well. When experiments do not produce the expected results, scientists sometimes take this as evidence against their theory, but sometimes they don't. Rather often, they continue working on the basis of their theory (T), even when they are aware of contrary evidence (~O). Second, the schema T→ P→ O oversimplifies the real nature of predictions. Theories never imply predictions all by themselves; they need background assumptions.

Imagine a nineteenth-century biologist seeking to test one of Pasteur's theories about germs. He collects blood samples from a healthy person and a person infected with some disease. He examines the samples under a microscope, expecting to see certain microorganisms in the second sample, but not in the first. But he does not find the expected germs. Does he announce a surprising refutation of Pasteur's theory? Before doing so, he might check to see if his microscope is working properly. The point of this rather homely example is that a particular prediction (P) is based not only on the theory (T) in question, but also on the basis of an indefinite number of background assumptions (B). The scientist assumes the microscope is working properly, and this involves assumptions about optics and microscope lenses; he assumes he has not mislabeled his samples; he assumes the symptoms of the disease seen in the patient indicate the patient really has the disease; and so on. So we need to change our schema for testing a theory.

$$(B + T) \rightarrow P \rightarrow O$$

Predictions are made on the basis of theory plus background assumptions. A negative observation (~O) does refute the prediction, but that does not necessarily refute the theory. This line of reasoning lies behind the Quine-Duhem thesis: no empirical observation ever refutes any scientific theory.[13] At most, a negative experimental result forces the scientist to make adjustments somewhere in her stock of beliefs. She may change her theory, but she may also change some background belief.

Notice that I have reverted to speaking about beliefs. What is the relationship between a scientist's beliefs and her theories? Should we say that scientists, or at least some of them, *believe* their theories? I think the answer is yes.

According to falsificationism, scientists always propose their hypotheses tentatively. Only after repeated failed attempts at falsifying a theory do scientists begin placing much confidence in a theory. The connotations of our words imply the change: *hypothesis* is not much more than a guess, while *theory* indicates a great deal more confidence. So say the falsificationists.

---

13. The Quine-Duhem thesis is named for two philosophers of science who independently emphasized this feature of the scientific enterprise: the American Willard V. O. Quine, and the Frenchman Pierre M. M. Duhem.

In reality, scientists sometimes have great confidence in their theories, even if they have not subjected them to many experimental tests. The fact of the matter is that scientists sometimes cling to their theory even in the face of contrary experimental evidence. The theory appeals to them because of its productiveness or comprehensiveness or beauty, and they are willing to seek adjustments in their background beliefs in order to accommodate contrary observations. In such cases I think it is appropriate to say that the scientist believes in the theory.[14] She will admit that the theory needs tweaking in this or that particular, but she is committed to the theory, especially in the sense that it directs her further scientific work.

Now, if a scientist believes the theory—and in the typical case she knows that other scientists in the field do not believe the theory—and if she is *for* the theory (she likes it, she defends it to others, she devises experiments based on it, etc.), then I submit that she has *faith* in the theory. I further contend that such faith often, though not always, helps the scientist achieve the goal of her practice: understanding. The reason for this is not hard to see. Scientific research, because it is a long-term social enterprise, presents scientists with many frustrations. A scientist has to stick with the work. She has to pursue lines of investigation that at some points are unpopular. She has to find a path into unknown territory. If the scientist continually changes her "research program" (to use the term of Imre Lakatos, a philosopher of science) or if she often changes her disciplinary "paradigm" (a term used by Thomas Kuhn, another philosopher of science), her work will never get anywhere. By exercising the virtue of faith in her theory, the scientist has a greater chance of success.

None of this, as stated, will be persuasive to the careful evidentialist. The careful evidentialist will say that a scientist *ought* to treat all her theoretical commitments as hypotheses only. To the extent that she actually does believe her theory, she is a bad scientist. But as I said earlier, this kind of stand prejudges the matter. We ought to look at particular cases. That matter I leave to chapter 5.

3.3 FAITH AS A VIRTUE IN SOCIAL AND POLITICAL REFORM

In an earlier work,[15] I have already proposed that we can consider politics a MacIntyrean practice. If we say that "politics" is the art and science of making group decisions—a definition specifically designed to include office

14. The case of Alfred Wegener in chapter 5 will illustrate all these features.

15. Smith, *Virtue of Civility in the Practice of Politics.*

politics, family politics, university politics, and church politics as well as public politics—then it seems obvious that the goal of politics is better decisions.[16] If we broadly define a "political opponent" as anyone who supports a competing proposal for the group, and if we realize that political opponents almost always know things we don't know, then it seems obvious that civility—a combination of habits and desires that motivate persons to treat political opponents well—is an important virtue in the practice of politics. Civility greatly improves communication between political opponents, which in turn greatly improves the odds of making better political decisions.

In the current context, I will use the same broad definition of politics (the art and science of making group decisions), but I will restrict my attention to public politics, which is the usual topic of political philosophy. It is still true, I submit, that the goal of politics is better decisions. Problems arise when we ask what it is that makes one political option better than another.

Political decisions in the public sphere aim at a number of not-always-compatible goods, including justice, wellbeing, and moral excellence. Philosophers have proposed a wide variety of political theories, and these theories define justice, the various elements of wellbeing, and moral excellence in different ways. Further, the competing theories rank the relative importance of these various goods differently. Even if we restrict ourselves to political philosophers who work explicitly in the context of liberal democracy, we still find competing conceptions of the most important goals of political decision-making. In short, political theory can be a wild and wooly business!

Practical life cannot wait for a resolution of all our theoretical questions. We should remind ourselves that political decisions are being made every day, and that we ourselves, by our actions or inaction, contribute to those decisions. Political theorists confront us with multiple, contradictory, and subtle claims about the goods we ought to pursue in political decisions. But we must not allow the existence of theoretical complexity and confusion to deter us from responsible participation in public politics.

Let us say that a "reformer" is a person who actively works for significant change in the social or political arrangements of society. I have in mind not only famous examples such as Martin Luther King Jr. or Mohandas Gandhi, but also ordinary people who get involved in efforts to change zoning ordinances, clean up pollution, build infrastructure (or prevent such building), criminalize certain behaviors (or decriminalize them), lower

---

16. Though I say this point is obvious, its implications are worth reflection. If the goal of politics is better decisions, then the goal of politics is not to have "my side" win. How often in our political discourse—on city commissions, on church boards, in corporate boardrooms, etc.—do we forget this?

taxes (or raise them), bring an end to a war, and so on. In both the famous and not so famous cases, the reformer has identified some feature of the current social or political situation that falls short of the ideal, at least as he perceives it. Put simply, the reformer believes "things could be better"—so he works to make things better.

Reformers are often motivated by concern for justice, as in the case of Martin Luther King Jr. They perceive the current situation as significantly unjust, so they labor for change. But other reformers aim not so much at rectifying injustice as at procuring some element of wellbeing for themselves or society as a whole; for instance, someone might campaign for funding for a public library or for some improvement in traffic safety. And some reformers aim at improving society morally; for example, campaigns against pornography or dog fighting. This last category—campaigns of moral reform—may not meet with much approval from political philosophers nowadays. Some might even see campaigns for moral reform as anti-liberal. But such judgments depend on certain conceptions of the requirements of a liberal social order, and those conceptions are themselves part of the "wild and wooly" debate in political philosophy. Historically, liberal democracies have seen reformers of all three sorts: those concerned for justice, those concerned for improving wellbeing, and those aimed at achieving moral excellence.

The ordinary citizen may not see himself as a reformer, but his participation in state politics will probably be driven by similar concerns. Suppose the citizen is considering voting for or against an initiative to raise the taxes on tobacco products in order to fund some public good. The public good—whether it is extending health insurance to people who don't have it, or something else—is a question of wellbeing. The citizen will have to estimate how far the proposed measure would improve the wellbeing of the intended beneficiaries. The citizen will also be concerned with questions of justice. Is it fair to tax one group (smokers) to provide a benefit for another group (the uninsured, only some of whom are smokers)? The citizen may also see the initiative as a way to punish the immoral behavior of tobacco company executives, that is, their long history of public lies and their calculated abuse of their customers. Somehow the citizen must weigh all these concerns against each other. And finally, the voter will also have to concern himself with practical and procedural questions—for instance, he might vote against one measure in hopes that a better option will come along; conversely, he might vote for the current flawed proposal as being better than nothing.

Philosophers might be tempted to suggest that the only way to sort through the complexities of the prior example (there are many others just as hard) is by means of a really good political theory. If that's true, liberal self-government faces the discouraging fact that few citizens have the inclination to read philosophy. On a more hopeful note, I suggest that political participation itself may train citizens to weigh these multiple concerns wisely. I don't say that it *will*; only that it *may*. Political experience may help some people become more perceptive and wise, while making others jaded and cynical.

We can now restate at least some of the internal goods of politics and social reform, conceived as MacIntyrean practices. These cooperative social activities aim at (1) producing a better understanding of central concepts relevant to social policy—concepts such as justice, wellbeing, human rights, autonomy, and virtue—*and* a better understanding of how these concepts can cohere, and (2) a better approximation of justice, wellbeing, and moral excellence in our actual social and political situation. Our political processes serve not only to change the world, but ideally they also serve to educate us about the goals toward which we try to bend our world.

How is faith a virtue in the practices of politics and reform? Precisely because political philosophy is unsettled and contentious, people are often confronted by other people who do not believe as they do about important political and social propositions. Obstacles and discouragements abound in the way of someone who works for better decisions in the state. It seems obvious that the campaigner/reformer who believes in the truth and value of his goal is more likely to persist in the pursuit of that goal than someone who merely wishes for the goal.

Some readers will object at this point: we already have too many fanatics, people who believe so strongly in their political goals that they are willing to trample other people and their goals in pursuit of them. If we say that faith is a virtue in politics and social reform, aren't we at the same time giving a pass to fanaticism?

No, we aren't, because faith is not the only virtue relevant to politics and social reform. I have already argued, in *The Virtue of Civility in the Practice of Politics*, that the citizen ought to strive for civility in the midst of political discourse (and discord). Clearly, then, I think there are at least two virtues, civility and faith, the possession of which tends to help persons involved in politics and reform achieve the internal goods of those practices. Surely, if we consider these practices carefully, we will find other virtues that facilitate success in politics and reform. Remember, success in politics is not winning, but achieving better decisions.

That there are multiple virtues relevant to success in politics and social reform underscores an important point about virtue ethics in general. We are not merely interested in understanding this or that virtue in isolation (as if such a thing were possible). We want to know how this or that virtue contributes to *a good life*, considered comprehensively. The MacIntyrean approach that I have adopted in this book directs our attention to the complex cooperative activities he calls practices, though as we saw in chapter 1, MacIntyre explicitly locates practices within the larger question of a unified life. One advantage of paying attention to practices is that we quickly discover that achieving the internal goods of practices requires multiple virtues. A so-called "faith" in a political goal that allows no room in a person's character for other important political virtues, such as civility, is actually a vice.[17] I will have more to say about the vices associated with faith in chapter 4.

For the present, let us assume that our reformer or campaigner has enough virtues present in his character to avoid fanaticism. If he is going to make progress toward the internal goods of politics or social reform, he must sometimes believe controversial propositions. He must sustain his belief in controversial propositions in the face of determined principled opposition from those who believe they already understand his position and have rejected it for what they think are good reasons. He must also sustain his belief when confronted by people who have no understanding and no desire to understand his position. And he must persist in his belief when his efforts are undermined by people who say they believe as he does but who actively resist any change in the political or social situation. In short, the effective reformer or campaigner needs faith.

3.4 FAITH AS A VIRTUE IN PARENTING

If we are concerned with living good lives, there can hardly be a more important practice than parenting children. After all, the good lives we hope to live are human lives, and human beings are radically dependent, social creatures.[18] If newborns do not receive care from other people they cannot possibly achieve good lives. And healthy adults are never more than an illness or accident from needing life-sustaining care from others. We all

17. My position here does not require that I believe in the so-called unity of the virtues. Going back to Plato, one strain of virtue theory has held that the virtues imply one another, so that if a person were to truly exhibit any particular virtue she would also have to have the others. I do not believe this. However, I think it is true that the possession of one virtue can greatly enhance other virtues in a person's character. And vices can greatly minimize the effectiveness of virtues in a person's character. My position in the text is only that in regard to a MacIntyrean practice, if a person has a character trait that *prevents* her from having a virtue relevant to achieving the internal goods of that practice, that character trait is a vice and not a virtue.

18. For an insightful discussion of human dependency, see MacIntyre, *Dependent Rational Animals*.

need caregivers. Therefore, we need an enormous supply of people who are morally and psychically able to give care to others, and the only way to get them is by raising children.

Our nature as dependent creatures gives us clues as to the goals of parenting. We want our children to be good human beings; at a minimum that means persons who are able to *receive* and *give* the care that dependent creatures need. We want more than the minimum; we want our children to be *excellent* human beings. That is, we want them to have all of the virtues necessary to flourish as human beings. Robert Adams points out that this means we wish not only moral virtues for our children, but also nonmoral excellences.[19]

I am not claiming that parents consciously aim at producing excellent human beings. In the day-to-day business of raising children, a parent is often focused on immediate challenges and responsibilities. The parent may well feel that she is bailing water so fast that there's no time to steer the boat. Furthermore, if a parent did have the luxury of thinking philosophically about the practice of parenting, she would encounter conflicting accounts of what constitutes human excellence: essentially the whole field of virtue ethics. Obviously, parents are not going to wait for philosophers to work out a satisfying virtue theory to tell them what to aim for in raising their children. Nevertheless, I think parents do aim, unconsciously perhaps, at human excellence.

We should take note of the asymmetrical relationship between parent and child. The parent aims at producing human excellence in the child; the child has no such goals for the parent. The practice of parenting, by its nature, reminds us that no human society will ever be a perfect egalitarian society, composed only of autonomous agents who freely contribute equally to all moral deliberation. Parents aim at producing human excellence *in someone else.* They may hope to develop virtues in themselves as they encounter the various struggles and opportunities of parenting, but the focus of their efforts *as parents* is on the child.

As I say, most parents probably do not think of their practice as aiming at the goal of human excellence. Parents plunge into the business of raising children armed mostly with moral platitudes and simple guidelines. They aim to *love* their children, provide them *care*, and *protect* them. Later, they try to *teach* their children, *discipline* them, and offer them *guidance.* Parents pick up moral guidelines from multiple sources: their own parents, social groups like mosques or synagogues, psychological professionals, and

---

19. Adams, *Theory of Virtue*, 26.

popular culture. Such guidelines can be coherent if they coalesce around a goal, even if that goal is never explicitly stated.

Is there a MacIntyrean "internal good" to the practice of parenting? I think there is. Though a parent may never explicitly affirm the goal of producing human excellence in another person, she will experience deep satisfaction—a satisfaction composed of pride, love, and joy—when she observes her child progressing toward that goal. In a happy case, this satisfaction occurs many times as the child grows, learns, and matures.

How does faith function as a virtue in parenting? In at least two ways, the second being more important than the first. First, because people have differing conceptions of human excellence, a parent may face "philosophical" challenges to her beliefs. She may become acutely aware that other people, for whom she has intellectual respect, explicitly reject some belief(s) she holds about the goals of parenting. Like a scientist who must stick with a research program in the face of supposedly disconfirming evidence, the parent must pursue her vision of human excellence even though she knows other people reject it. If she repeatedly changes her ideals, she will likely only confuse her child.

Second and more important, parents often encounter failure and discouragement as they seek to build human excellence in their children. A parent may be tempted to despair when she considers the powerful forces that work against her project. For instance, in the United States today a parent who wishes her child to learn *contentment* faces the challenge of a consumerist culture and its nearly ubiquitous advertising presence. The parent who wants to raise a *peaceable* child faces militarism and the glorification of violence in entertainment. The parent who aims for a *self-disciplined* child must overcome the siren song of the drug culture. And so on: parents rightly worry about how their children will be affected by street crime, poverty, racial prejudice, divorce, and other problems.

Now, if a parent ceases to believe that her project can succeed—that is, if she despairs over her child—she may abandon the effort. A parent needs to believe that her efforts for her child are worthwhile, even when there is precious little evidence of progress toward human excellence in the child (and even when the child demands or begs that the parent abandon the child). These beliefs, held in the face of counterevidence, are faith. It seems obvious that such faith tends to help parents achieve the internal goods of parenting. It fortifies them against despair in the hard times, which makes possible the satisfaction of the good times.

Remember that in chapter 2 we imagined a possible objection along these lines. Maybe all we need for success in our practices is to *feel* and *act* in a certain way; we don't really need to *believe*. As I pointed out there, a loosely Freudian view of the mind—any psychology according to which the unconscious mind plays a significant role in our behavior—undermines this objection. If the parent really does not believe that her child can escape the lure of the gang, she will despair. And children are extremely adept at picking up on their parents' fears.

3.5 SUMMARY OF THE ARGUMENT

A virtue, I said in chapter 1, is an acquired characteristic of human beings the possession of which tends to help people gain the internal goods of practices. Faith, I said in chapter 2, combines believing and being for something that is not believed by persons for whom the believer has intellectual respect. In the current chapter I have briefly examined three important practices: scientific research, social and political reform, and parenting. In each case, I argue, we find that faith as defined helps us achieve plausible internal goods of the practice. Therefore faith is a virtue.

4

⟨⌒⟩

The Vice of Credulity

So far I have argued that faith is a virtue because it contributes to success in important human practices: research, reform, and parenting.
Some readers may be happy to agree with this thesis and eager to move on
to a more contentious issue: religious faith. But other readers will have noticed holes in the argument. They may think I have left unaddressed certain
points that ought to be clarified. Or some things I have said may seem to
imply conclusions that cannot be true, so I should explain how to avoid such
apparent implications.

I must disappoint both groups of readers. I will not discuss religious
faith until chapter 8, partly because there *are* holes in the argument as it
has been presented so far. I will try in this chapter to mend some of them.
However, I will certainly not repair all the weaknesses in the argument to
this point, for a very good reason: I don't know what they are. The best I can
do is address some of the problems of which I am aware.

For instance, someone might think, given the drift of the book so far,
that I think the evidentialist brief against faith is simply stupid, a hopeless
error caused by animus against religion. True, some philosophers' work has
been motivated by hatred of religion, but I think the evidentialist worry
points to a genuine problem. The primary goal of this chapter is to discuss
what is right in evidentialism, as I see it.

4.1 CREDULITY: BELIEVING TOO READILY

Some people allege that Jesus had Mary Magdalene as his wife. It is safe to say that many people believe this, due to the influence and popularity of *The Da Vinci Code*. Other people were convinced by Oliver Stone's *JFK* that a conspiracy was responsible for President Kennedy's assassination.

But people ought to critically examine such claims. As a university professor, I try in my teaching both to show students how to criticize propositions like these and to motivate them to do work that stands up to critical analysis. This is standard stuff in philosophy and liberal arts education generally. The critical mind asks for evidence, precision, and coherence. A properly educated person will incorporate these standards into her character.

Notice that when we speak of incorporating "standards" into a person's "character," we enter, once again, the realm of the virtues. The critical examination of propositions is a virtuous activity, a good thing. It is part of a good life. Yet it is only a *part*; there is more to life than the critical examination of beliefs. And it is part of a *good life*, that is, a life lived according to a moral vision. Some educators are hesitant to think in these terms; they don't want to admit that they are training their students in virtues, and they may be particularly averse to the notion of a "good life," since it sounds narrow, conformist, and authoritarian. I mentioned Alasdair MacIntyre's recursive description of the good life for human beings in chapter 1, and it is helpful here. An essential part of the good life for human beings is the ongoing effort to understand what the good life for human beings is. Whatever other elements it includes, the good life should be marked by growth in understanding and deepening of perspective. Educators can freely confess that their work has moral substance without buying into anti-liberal authoritarianism.

Aristotle introduced the notion of the golden mean. On his account, virtues typically lie somewhere between two vices. For instance, if we define distributive justice as giving to persons the rewards they deserve, we can miss this goal by giving someone too little or too much. Even if we use the same word, *injustice,* to describe both failings, Aristotle said we should recognize them as different. The injustice of giving too small a reward is unfair to the person who receives it, and the injustice of giving too great a reward is unfair to other people, who feel cheated.

Aristotle thought the golden mean applied to moral virtues across the board. In each case, true virtue lay somewhere between the vice of excess and the vice of deficit. Courage is the quintessential virtue of the soldier, who must do his duty in the face of danger. If the soldier runs away from danger, he exhibits the vice of deficit, and we say he shows cowardice. But if the soldier is too eager to face danger—we can imagine him running ahead of his comrades in his eagerness to engage the enemy—he is guilty of the vice of excess, which we call foolhardiness.

I think we can apply Aristotle's doctrine to the subject of this book. We have been considering situations of belief, situations in which people ponder doubtful propositions. A person can miss a properly critical attitude in either of two ways: by believing too readily or by being too slow or un- willing to believe. I will call these opposite vices credulity and skepticism. Examples of credulity: credulous persons too quickly and too readily believe that Kennedy was the victim of a conspiracy, that Jesus was married, that Saddam Hussein's Iraq was connected to the 9/11 attacks, or that herbal remedies cure cancer.

When I say that there is something right in evidentialism, it is because credulity is a real vice. The shipowner in W. K. Clifford's fable convinced himself that his ship would sail safely, and his belief was credulous. The shipowner believed too quickly and easily; checking on the seaworthiness of his ship would only have cost him time and money. Clifford rightly insisted that the shipowner's *sincerity* could not excuse his immoral believing. Now the moral of the story, according to Clifford, is a prohibition—"it is wrong always, everywhere, and for anyone, to believe anything upon insufficient evidence"—and I have already argued that Clifford's prohibition is over- stated. Nevertheless, it will be worth our while to pay attention to credulity.

On the whole, philosophers are more likely to exhibit skepticism than credulity. In chapter 3, I described evidentialism as a moral doctrine preaching a *rule*, either E or E2. Another way to think about evidentialism is to regard the evidentialists' doctrine as an attempt to describe the proper *virtue* for those situations in which we ponder doubtful propositions. The proper virtue, evidentialists might say, is *proper criticism*, and a questioning attitude is the whole of the virtue. However, since Clifford famously and influentially expressed the evidentialist doctrine as a moral rule, in chapter 3 I treated evidentialism as a rule rather than an attempted description of virtue.

If credulity is being too willing or eager to believe something, we might think that our first job is to formulate a rule for right believing. This would be to draw a line in the epistemic dirt, so to speak. Epistemic virtue would then consist in not stepping over the line. I think this is the wrong approach. I am deliberately using the language of virtue and vice to discuss epistemological issues.[1] Rather than fall back into a discussion of rules or

---

1. I am following Linda Zagzebski and several other philosophers who have urged us to think in terms of virtue epistemology; see Zagzebski, *Virtues of the Mind*. See also Roberts and Wood, *Intellectual Virtues*.

decision procedures, I think we ought to stick to the conceptual array of virtue and vice.

Besides giving us the notion of the golden mean, Aristotle made observations about the process of acquiring virtues. The first step in learning a virtue is to see it in others. Even this first step requires some moral training; we need to learn that there is such a thing as courage or open-mindedness so we can look for it. Further, we may need to learn about vices of deficit and excess: one can miss courage by falling into either cowardice or foolhardiness, and we can miss open-mindedness by being closed to others' ideas or by adopting whichever opinion we learned most recently.

Obviously, it is not enough to know about virtue or to recognize it in others. Aristotle said that we habituate ourselves to virtue by mimicking the behavior of virtuous people. Early on in the process of learning a virtue, we may experience *akrasia*, Aristotle's label for the person who knows the right thing to do but does not do it. Imagine an Athenian conscript soldier thrown into his first battle. He knows, intellectually, that he ought to exhibit courage in the face of danger, and he knows also the particular duties he ought to fulfill on the battle line. Nevertheless, in the heat of the battle, the draftee runs from danger. This is *akrasia*. Even though the draftee exhibits the vice of cowardice, Aristotle thought *akrasia* was a step up from simple viciousness, because this soldier at least recognizes his fault and aspires to overcome it.

In the next stage of virtue acquisition, a person forces himself to do what he should through self-control. In the case of our imagined Athenian conscript, there may come a time when he continues to feel fear in the presence of danger, but he overcomes his inclination to run away. In a battle situation he might literally mimic the movements of brave soldiers.

I submit that *akrasia* and self-control apply to the acquisition of intellectual virtues too.[2] Someone could recognize and admire open-mindedness in others but continue to act in closed-minded ways— for example, by reading only those political columnists who, she knows, support her own positions. This would be intellectual *akrasia*. She might then copy the behavior of some open-minded person she admires and compel herself to read or listen to "enemy" ideas, and this would be intellectual self-control.

Over time, with more practice, the soldier gradually finds it easier to do his duty. His knowledge of the danger involved in battle does not decrease; if anything, it grows. His fear has not disappeared, but he has learned to manage it. We can imagine that new feelings, a sense of competence and confidence, now accompany his experience of battle. The person learning

---

2. Zagzebski persuades me on this point (*Virtues of the Mind*, 154–55).

open-mindedness may come to feel pleasure in considering contrary ideas. At the end of the process, Aristotle thought, the person can be said to truly have the virtue, an established habit or pattern that involves feeling, thinking, and behaving. We need not require that the virtuous person act in accord with the virtue on every occasion; it is enough if she has developed a dependable pattern of behavior.[3]

I find Aristotle's account of learning virtue appealing in several respects. He emphasizes psychological and experiential aspects of virtue, and his story makes room for complexity (beliefs, emotions, and behaviors mutually influence each other) and the fact that we acquire habits bit by bit. In a similar way, I want to talk about psychological and experiential aspects of the vice of credulity.

It's much easier to fall into vice than be trained in virtue.[4] Nevertheless, habituation applies to vice as much as to virtue. Repetition makes it easier and easier to maintain character traits, whether those traits are vicious or virtuous. Suppose we say that some feeling or behavior tends to lead persons into credulity. We should not be as concerned with isolated incidences of

---

3. How dependable does a pattern of behavior have to be in order to conclude that a person has a virtue? Some researchers in social psychology have questioned the whole concept of a virtue, claiming that differences in situation are far better predictors of behavior than the character traits of agents. The claims of the "situationists" are too complicated to discuss in detail here. Robert Adams gives a helpful discussion of this question in *Theory of Virtue*, 115–43. However, I will make a few comments.

Suppose we grant that situational factors play a greater role in moral agents' behavior than individual character. For example, research might show that the perceived risk of being found out might correlate better with honest answers on tests than the test takers' virtue of honesty or dishonesty (established independently). This is not enough to show that the difference between the honest and dishonest test takers is not real. We typically like to think of the honest person answering truthfully in all or almost all situations. The social psychological research of the situationists might force us to conclude that virtues are more like tendencies than performance guarantees. But even "mere tendencies" might be well worth our attention. By analogy, consider two baseball players, a major league star hitter and a major league benchwarmer. If they were inserted into a Little League game, both would get hits almost all the time. When they are inserted into a major league game, both get hits far less than half the time. Situational factors seem to correlate better with their hitting than does their difference in ability. Yet that difference is real. It is the measurable tendency that makes the star a better player than the benchwarmer in real major league situations.

Suppose, then, that situational factors do correlate better with the actual behavior of agents than their character traits. So long as the honest person has a greater tendency toward honest behavior than the dishonest person, I would argue that there is a significant moral difference between them.

4. How do I know that vice is easier than virtue? By experience, I suppose. Perhaps others' experience contradicts mine. How fortunate for them!

that feeling or behavior as we should be concerned with repeated and consistent feeling or behavior.

What feeds credulity? No one sets out to be a fool. What factors push people to want to believe, with the result that they believe too readily? I will suggest five possible culprits, without any implication that my list is complete.

First, credulity can be associated with simple naiveté. Young persons, people whose experiences are limited to small social groups, people who read little, people without means to travel from their places of birth—such people may believe too readily simply because they don't see that there are alternatives. To one degree or another, we are all naïve. We believe things—rather, we live as if certain things were true—without ever so much as noticing them.[5]

Second, sometimes credulity flows from sheer laziness, the old-fashioned vice of sloth. It takes work to properly investigate many questions. In regard to the Kennedy assassination, you might need to read the Warren Commission's report or other sources. You may need to learn how to distinguish good sources from bad ones.[6] In some cases a proper investigation may be as simple as asking wise persons what they think about the matter. Whether the labor of investigation is extensive and difficult or relatively easy, laziness tempts us to shirk it. Then, since the person hasn't done the work needed to believe responsibly, he slips into believing irresponsibly. Irresponsible believing could be expressed as an unwillingness to believe, as when South African politicians publicly doubted that HIV causes AIDS or when North American politicians publicly doubted that burning fossil fuels contributes to a planetary greenhouse effect. That is to say, laziness can provoke skepticism. But irresponsible believing often appears as credulity, as when one believes some idea because a popular movie endorsed it.

Third, credulity often stems from our desire for social approval. The social unit may be the family, the village, the school, a business, a union, the nation, or a church. Human beings band together in many ways, and in virtually all of these attachments we desire the approbation of others. We learn to "fit in" by means of our dress, speech, mannerisms, and many other ways, including our beliefs. Some groups exert explicit pressure on individuals to believe properly, as in religious groups or the thought control

---

5. G. E. Moore's propositions of common sense come to mind. For instance: I have lived my whole life very near the surface of the earth.

6. With the advent of ubiquitous Internet access, teaching students to distinguish reputable scholarship from nonsense has become more important than ever.

of totalitarian states. Other times, the pressure for right belief is subtler, as in political discourse on university campuses.[7]

Fourth, desire for closure in intellectual matters also motivates credulity. Here the pressure stems more from individual psychology than from social forces. Some persons experience uncertainty as disorienting or dismaying. Most of us, I think, experience some discomfort when confronted with uncertainty—especially when some previously unquestioned belief comes under scrutiny for the first time, or when one discovers inconsistency between two of her beliefs that she hadn't noticed before. For some, uncertainty causes significant distress. If the discomfort is great enough, individuals may flee the psychic pain by seizing a quick resolution: "The butler did it." The solution may be correct—maybe the butler did do it—but the belief is still vicious, because the believer committed herself to the belief too readily.

A fifth motive for credulity is desire for novelty. This is related to the desire for social approval. But now the credulous person believes some proposition not because others in the group already believe it but because they do not and because he wants to impress them. My miracle story is even more wonderful than yours is! Of course Jesus was married, but that isn't the half of it—let me tell you more!

Virtually all people desire to feel important. We want to fit in, but we also want to be significant, even if it is only by being the first on our block to own the new toy or believe the new thing. That is why both social desires— the desire to believe like others and the desire to believe just a little more than others—can push us to believe too readily.

As I said, I don't think these are the only feelings or desires that push us into credulity. Readers can add to the list.[8] But I have said enough to show that a variety of motives can lead to vice.

Remember, the vice of credulity consists of a pattern, not a single instance, of overreadiness to believe. Probably everyone jumps to unwarranted conclusions sometimes. We want to guard against making it a habit. How do we do that?

---

7. I do not by this comment take a side in debates between left and right in campus politics. The point is that persons often feel pressure to believe one way or another because they desire group approval. Since a liberal education includes explicit efforts to inculcate critical thinking, some people in universities may think that their schools have somehow inoculated students against such pressures. It's not so, and the more we congratulate ourselves on having achieved a neutral discourse, the more we deceive ourselves.

8. One reader suggested that some people want to differentiate from their group; they may succumb to credulity because they want to *escape* from their social group and *believing more* provides a break from the group. I thank Ron Davis for this suggestion.

4.2 THE CURE FOR CREDULITY

Throughout this discussion, we must resist the tempting question, Well, what is the definition of believing too readily? Philosophers often hanker for a tidy definition, spelled out in terms of necessary and sufficient conditions, for right believing. If we surrender to this desire, we will imagine that proper believing will be achieved by following certain rules. In contrast, the conceptual framework of virtue and vice helps steer us back to matters of habituation. Of course, it is possible in some situations to acquire a new habit by consciously and repeatedly acting in accord with a rule. More often, though, I suggest that Aristotle's observations about virtue acquisition point us in a better direction. We habituate ourselves to virtue by mimicking the behavior of others.[9]

I will illustrate by considering the causes of credulity listed in 4.1. First, against naiveté, we notice that wise persons open themselves to learning. We see them reading new books. We hear them discussing new ideas. By watching wise persons we realize that an essential component of wisdom is the continuing search for wisdom. Again: we need to *notice*, to *pay attention.* Here I borrow ideas from Iris Murdoch's emphases in moral philosophy.[10] Murdoch argued that philosophers often wrongly assume that ethics is about making decisions, when actually our behavior is often driven by the way we perceive the world around us. Evil, she said, usually does not arise from a willful determination to harm others (though that is possible), but from a kind of indifference, when we don't do the hard work of paying attention.

Second, against laziness, we notice that wise persons practice intellectual discipline. They work. They go to class, metaphorically as well as literally. They learn how to do real scholarship, and they put their scholarly skills into practice.

---

9. Do we learn virtue *only* by imitating others? Are there no "moral pioneers"? Given the MacIntyrean definition of virtue used in this book, the answer must be: it's possible that there are. Human beings are creative; over time, they invent new practices. It is possible that some new practices may require new virtues to allow people to gain the internal goods of those practices. However, since any new practice will be a "cooperative human activity," some well-recognized virtues will always be appropriate, such as honesty and courage.

10. Some readers will be familiar with Iris Murdoch as the author of *Under the Net* and many other novels. Others will have seen the film *Iris*, based on the memoirs of her husband, John Bailey. Beyond writing novels, Murdoch produced several important works in moral philosophy, including *Sovereignty of Good* and *Metaphysics as a Guide to Morals*. For a helpful summary of Murdoch's moral philosophy, see Widdows, *Moral Vision of Iris Murdoch*.

Let me be clear. I do not mean to suggest that all wise persons are academics. As a teacher, I have the privilege of rubbing shoulders with people whose intellectual hard work is of that type. But we can observe intellectual discipline in places other than the academy: the civil servant who offers the planning commission advice based on careful research, the middle manager who takes the time to converse with the workers under his authority so that he really knows how things are going on the factory floor, the salesperson who learns about her competitors' products as well as her company's line, and so on. These people display intellectual discipline as much as the professor.

Third, against social conformity, we notice that wise persons have intellectual courage. Alasdair MacIntyre noted that courage will be a necessary virtue in any vital intellectual tradition, because a living tradition needs people to raise challenges to accepted ideas. Otherwise, the tradition stagnates.[11] Obviously, wise persons do not challenge everything in their tradition. That's not possible, since if a revolutionary rejects everything in the tradition, he is no longer reforming it but abandoning it. When Martin Luther rebelled against the authority of the church, he did so as a Christian and he defended his reforms by appealing to Christian texts. When Albert Einstein proposed the theory of relativity, he did not refute Newtonian physics; rather, he showed how Newtonian physics was a particular kind of physics subsumed under a more comprehensive theory. Luther and Einstein illustrated intellectual courage by their willingness to stand for change. It's also possible that courage may be needed to resist change in a tradition. Either way, there is a price to be paid, and wise persons are willing to bear the costs of nonconformity at the right time.

Fourth, against the comfort of premature closure, we notice that wise persons have trained themselves to tolerate the discomfort of uncertainty. They do not rejoice in uncertainty or make skepticism their goal, but they are able to live without commitments in regard to some questions, even questions that other people find pressing.

Fifth, against the desire for novelty, we notice that wise persons have learned contentment. They know that it is okay to be who they are; they don't need to impress others by the oddity of their beliefs.

In running through my list of motives for credulity and my list of antidotes, I run the risk of making things sound simple when they aren't. For instance, someone might object to an illustration I used a few pages back. I spoke disparagingly of North American politicians who do not believe in global warming; I mentioned this as an example of the vice of skepticism.

11. MacIntyre, *After Virtue*, 223.

The objector might argue that the case for anthropogenic global warming is not strong.[12] It would be better, the objector might say, to learn to tolerate uncertainty. If human activities really are causing climate change, the matter certainly deserves our attention—but we ought to beware that the very urgency of the question might motivate us to believe too quickly.

We recognize, then, that we have conflicting motives. On one hand, a person might want to believe in global warming in order to fit in with his group. (He might not, depending on which social group is important to him.) On another hand, he might not want to believe in global warming because he opposes certain economic or political implications of that belief. Some of our motives push us toward one vice, credulity, while others push us toward another vice, skepticism. So things are complicated, not simple. Is there a way forward?

Yes. I have said repeatedly that we notice wise persons. We pay attention to people around us. When we recognize admirable traits in others, we can begin the business of incorporating those traits into ourselves. Naturally, we should not try to achieve greater precision in our description of proper critical thinking than the matter allows—yet another of Aristotle's insights. We observe that wise persons do not agree on all points; in every field of inquiry wise people sometimes disagree pointedly about specific questions. So we ought to pay attention to many exemplars rather than one or two. And we look for habits and patterns of attitude and practice rather than judgments about specific questions.

Perhaps I can make my main point clearer by comparing my comments here to the famous passage in Francis Bacon's *Novum Organum* where he describes the "idols of the mind." Bacon was a late sixteenth/early seventeenth-century philosopher, statesman, and scientist who enthusiastically advocated a turn to empirical science. Bacon accused people in his day of all sorts of irresponsible believing, and he identified various psychological causes that produced faulty beliefs. Bacon labeled these causes of error "idols of the mind" and described four classes of them.

The first group, the "idols of the tribe," belongs to the whole human "tribe," so to speak. Bacon thought intellectual faults like oversimplification or the tendency to be overly impressed by flashy examples were nearly universal in the human race. Items in the second group, the "idols of the cave," were more individual. One person may err by focusing too much on detail, while another may err by focusing only on the big picture.

---

12. The Internet supplies many examples of people (with varying scientific credentials) who deny anthropogenic global warming. For a listing, see www.globalwarming-skeptics.info.

Third, the "idols of the marketplace" arise from human interaction, which takes place via language. Bacon, like many other philosophers before and after him, thought that we are often led astray by accidental features of our language. For instance, we have different words for steam, water, and ice, so we may fail to see the underlying unifying nature of these things. Or whales and sharks might be lumped together as "fish," when their real natures are very different.

Fourth, the "idols of the theatre" are false philosophical theories. Like other philosophers of the early modern period, Bacon harshly criticized medieval scholasticism. Scholasticism focused far too much, Bacon thought, on preserving ancient knowledge—as if everything worth knowing was already recorded in the Bible or in Aristotle. Real scholarship should focus on gaining new knowledge and should be willing to overturn the tradition when it was shown to be wrong.

What I have said about factors that motivate credulity and what Bacon said about the idols of the mind are similar in this respect: we are both attempting to understand the *experience* of believing (epistemological psychology, one might call it) and finding things that go wrong. Our diagnoses use different terms, but they aren't opposed.

Bacon and I differ, though, in our proposed treatments. Bacon urged us to move to scientific empiricism (though his own understanding of scientific method was limited). That is, his solution was to turn to *method*. Bacon is the father of those who think our epistemological problems will be solved by proper procedure.

I hope it is clear I have nothing against scientific empiricism. If we want to believe responsibly when it comes to greenhouse gasses and global warming, obviously we should ask the scientists.

Nevertheless, I urge us not to seek a rule for right believing. (Certainly not this rule: "Believe only what scientific empirical research supports.") Having identified problems in epistemological psychology, I don't think the answer is to be found in proper procedure alone. Rather, I suggest that we identify and train ourselves in epistemological virtue. This means paying attention to wise persons around us. And when our topic is intellectual vice, including the vice of credulity, again we should pay attention to examples.

4.3 ON FINDING EXAMPLES

By examples, I mean exemplars—wise persons and credulous persons. We will not and do not need to agree on all the examples. The wise persons I admire and try to emulate may include authors whom you also admire—thus the importance of good reading. But many of the exemplars of wisdom I admire will be people unknown to you (nonauthors, most likely), and those you emulate may be unknown to me. Similarly with vice: the credulous people I see and try not to emulate will not likely be the fools you suffer.

Someone might ask: how do we know we are training ourselves in the same virtue (or guarding against the same vice) if our respective stocks of exemplars overlap so little? For example, I said above that wise persons have trained themselves to tolerate uncertainty, and this helps guard against premature closure in questions of belief. But surely this is a matter of degree; not all people we may regard as wise will exhibit the same tolerance for uncertainty. How much is enough?

Once again the desire for a neat definition rises up, when a vague definition is all we need. We have said that credulity is the overreadiness to believe. If you and I both observe numerous examples of credulous believers, then pay attention to the psychological and experiential factors exhibited by such cases, and finally try to guide our epistemological development by avoiding such bad examples, we will make progress.

But what about contradictory exemplars? We might imagine an evidentialist objecting that *no* exemplar exhibiting religious faith should be counted as an example of virtuous believing. Religious persons are by definition credulous, this objector might say. We could also imagine the opposite objection offered by a believer: atheists (maybe agnostics too) are *always* guilty of skepticism. Both extremes could object to my neo-Aristotelian project of learning virtue by mimicking wise persons by saying that we need to settle first on a definition of right believing and a method for achieving it.

Against this objection I will mount a fairly simple empirical defense. Like Socrates, I don't need to persuade the crowd, but only you, the reader. Consider your own case. Is it actually true that the people for whom you have intellectual respect are only of one sort? That is, you know *no one* with religious faith who also exhibits intellectual self-control, curiosity, open-mindedness, and so forth? For those at the other extreme: is it true that you know *no* nonbelievers who are able to commit themselves to worthy practices (such as research science, social reform, or parenting) and to incorporate these practices into good lives?

I suspect that anyone who has read this far in this book will admit that he knows intellectually admirable people on both sides of the theist/atheist fault line. Or to speak more accurately: the readers of this book *would* recognize such examples if they were accustomed to looking for virtuous people. As a matter of fact, many people don't pay much attention to examples. They have been trained by their families, schools, or religious groups to think about both morality and epistemology in terms of rules. Do this; don't do that. Form your beliefs this way; do not form them any other way.

I am not urging that we completely abandon moral or epistemological rules. Certainly rules like "do not murder" have a place in practical morality. But I am urging that we shift the weight of our attention to virtues and exemplars. We ought to pay attention to real people we admire and learn to be like them. Applied to the question of believing doubtful things, we ought to pay attention to real people whose ability to handle doubtful matters contributes to living good lives.

If we do this, it is highly unlikely that we will come up with wildly different and opposing pictures of credulity. The fact that I could list five factors that feed credulity and that you could agree that all or most of them really do play the roles I described in feeding credulity allays the worry that my vice is your virtue. The goal is not to achieve a precise definition, but to grow in one's love for wisdom. Iris Murdoch wrote that moral philosophers ought to ask how we can make ourselves morally better.[13] It is not enough to strive to understand moral concepts; we want to improve. Following Aristotle, I have suggested a way to do that.

4.4 ADDENDUM: ON ETHICS AND EPISTEMOLOGY

In chapter 3 I stressed that the evidentialists' rule against believing anything on insufficient evidence is a moral rule. I have claimed that the argument of this book is a moral argument rather than an epistemological argument. Readers might conclude that I think ethics (moral philosophy) and epistemology (theory of knowledge) are thoroughly distinct things. I do not. Rather, I think there is significant overlap between ethics and epistemology. If there is such an overlap, I need to explain why I think I can argue that faith is a virtue while leaving unanswered many questions in epistemology.

One way to think about this matter is to ask about the aims of ethics and epistemology. Ethics aims to explain the "good" and the "right." Moral philosophers differ as to which of these concepts is more fundamental, but usually they try to give some account of both. What, if anything, is intrinsically excellent? In particular, what excellences are appropriate for human beings? What is the right thing to do? Why are certain behaviors morally right, whereas others are morally wrong? I suggest that all of these questions can be lumped together; we can think of them as the theoretical side of ethics. But ethics also has a practical side, which seeks to tell us how to do the right thing and by doing the right thing how to become better persons.

13. Murdoch, *Sovereignty of Good*, 52.

Epistemology has a similar structure. It aims, on a theoretical level, to understand what knowledge is. Under what conditions can we say that a person knows something? What is the relationship between belief and knowledge? Between understanding and knowledge? Additionally, on the practical level, epistemology seeks to tell us how to acquire knowledge. One might characterize Michael Polanyi's vision of epistemology as a determination to pursue the practice question without letting the theoretical question get in the way.

On the theoretical level, the two fields seem very distinct. Ethics aims to explain the good and the right, while epistemology aims to explain knowledge. But at the practical level ethics and epistemology overlap, because both aim to tell us what to do. They both give rules, advices, and decision procedures—and they both recommend virtues.

Examples might help. In ethics, a rule might be this: "Be consistent: treat similar cases similarly, and different cases differently." A bit of ethical advice might be, "Be alert to the needs of the poor." A formal decision procedure could be found in the methods of a hospital ethics review board. And courage is often offered as an example of moral virtue. In epistemology, a rule might be this: "Never believe anything on insufficient evidence." An advice might be, "Learn from the methods of successful scientists." Decision procedures can be found in formal research reports. Curiosity or open-mindedness could be suggested as examples of epistemological virtues.[14]

In this book, I am trying to recommend faith as a virtue. To do so I have had to give an account of what faith is and explain how faith, so understood, contributes to the good life. Epistemological questions present themselves because faith, as I have described it, involves belief, and the practical side of epistemology often addresses belief.

I don't think I need to give a satisfying theoretical account of what knowledge is and how it is connected to related concepts like belief and understanding in order to defend a piece of practical moral philosophy. If I want to defend a moral rule or recommend a virtue, I ought to do so in the light of a satisfying account of moral concepts. This is why I began, in chapter 1, with a general discussion of virtue. Now, if some piece of practical epistemology (e.g., a rule such as the evidentialist rule) *conflicts* with the bit of practical moral philosophy under consideration, what should we do? If the conflict is irreconcilable, we will have to give up one advice or the other, but we ought to at least hope that practical morality and practical epistemology can coexist. We might need to reexamine our thinking on both topics.

14. I write as if moral virtues and intellectual virtues are distinct classes, as Aristotle thought they were. However, see Zagzebski's rejection of any hard boundary between moral and epistemological virtues (*Virtues of the Mind*, 137–58).

We certainly ought to be wary of attempts by either side to preemptively disallow seemingly good conclusions from the other field.

The evidentialists offer their rule as a guide to knowledge, but they freely admit—as we have seen, they insist—that it is also a moral rule. Their rule leaves no room to recognize faith as a virtue. But I have argued that faith contributes to good living by helping us achieve the internal goods of important practices. Obviously, I think we ought not to accept the evidentialist rule in either the extreme form (E) or the more careful form (E2).[15] Either form of the rule is a bit of epistemological imperialism; these rules simply refuse to countenance the conclusion that faith is a virtue.

Ethical imperialism would be just as bad as epistemological imperialism. Suppose I have given a sound argument and faith really is a virtue. I should not, for that reason, simply ignore the reasons evidentialists have for urging their rule. If the argument of chapter 3 is sound, neither E nor E2 can be straightforwardly true, but they may nevertheless point to something important. What they point to is the danger of credulity.

It might help to ask the question, how is the evidentialist rule supposed to aid us in the search for knowledge? "Never believe anything on insufficient evidence" or "Never believe anything more strongly than the evidence indicates"—the rule seems to aim at excluding certain beliefs. I think we should readily admit that excluding certain beliefs is a necessary part of epistemology's practical side.

Consider what desires we have in regard to belief. We want to believe the truth, but that's not enough. If believing true propositions were our only aim, the safest course would be to believe every proposition (if this were possible, which it isn't), because then we would be sure to believe all the true ones. We have to balance our desire to believe truths with an equally important desire not to believe falsehoods. Further, we desire to believe the truth about important matters. A person could spend a great deal of time and energy adding to her stock of trivial, but true, beliefs by carefully charting the position of each blade of grass in her lawn. Her life would be better if she used that time and energy in other ways, perhaps studying botany. She might acquire fewer true beliefs, but they would be more important.

Among our epistemological desires, evidentialism tries to help us with the second desire just mentioned; it aims to guard against believing false things. Surely that is a worthy concern. We address that concern by learning to avoid credulity. While avoiding credulity, we want also to escape the

---

15. To save the reader paging back to chapter 3: (E) It is wrong always, everywhere, and for anyone, to believe anything upon insufficient evidence; and (E2) It is wrong always, everywhere, and for anyone, to believe things *which are not believed by persons for whom one has intellectual respect* upon insufficient evidence.

opposite vice, skepticism. And the way to do both, I suggest, is to pay attention to examples. So in the next three chapters, we turn to real cases.

5

Faith as a Virtue
in Scientific Research

Philosophers, perhaps because they often think about abstract problems, frequently use imagined examples to illustrate their ideas. So far in this book I've invented Elaine, who believes a hurricane will hit her county; Sheryl, who wants to be an architect; an unnamed dishonest architect and an equally dishonest builder; and other minor characters such as our Athenian soldier. Using imagined examples is better than using no examples at all; without them philosophical writing might be unreadable.

But now we come to a point where imagined examples simply will not do. In the previous chapter I urged that we pay attention to exemplars, real people who exhibit the virtues we would like to build into our own character. Conversely, we ought also to pay attention to people whose vices we hope to avoid. Therefore I plan to present case studies in this and the two subsequent chapters that illustrate and partially corroborate my main thesis.

5.1 THE ARGUMENT RESTATED

By now readers are familiar with the main argument of this book. First premise: a virtue is an acquired human characteristic the possession of which helps human beings achieve the internal goods of practices. Second premise: faith is an acquired human characteristic the possession of which helps people achieve the internal goods of three important practices, namely, scientific research, political and social reform, and parenting. Conclusion: faith is a virtue.

The exemplars in this chapter illustrate two of the uses of "faith" listed in chapter 2. Henrietta Leavitt illustrates faith$_{(7)}$; Alfred Wegener is an example of faith$_{(8)}$. Strictly speaking, then, only the second exemplar supports the thesis of the book, because my conclusion is that faith$_{(8)}$ is a virtue. Nevertheless, it will be instructive to compare the two cases; they help us see what Wittgenstein called "family resemblances" between our concepts.

5.2 THE CASE OF HENRIETTA LEAVITT

We don't know enough about Henrietta Leavitt. She left no diary, and the relatively few letters she wrote to Edward Pickering (which are catalogued at Harvard) give us only hints of what was going on in her life. George Johnson wrote a short biography of Henrietta Leavitt, and he did the best he could with limited materials, but more than half that book is devoted to explaining the significance of Leavitt's discovery.[1] Thus, the reader should be put on notice: I will be tempted to overinterpret what we do know about Leavitt. But her work is so interesting that I will run the risk.

5.2.1 Leavitt's Life

Henrietta Swan Leavitt was born July 4, 1868, in Lancaster, Massachusetts, and was named after her mother, Henrietta Swan (Kendrick) Leavitt. Her father, George Roswell Leavitt, was a Congregationalist pastor. The couple had seven children—four girls and three boys. It was an age of large families and high infant mortality; Henrietta, the oldest child, lost both a brother and a sister in their toddlerhood.

Ministerial families tend to move from parish to parish. In 1880 the Leavitts were in Cambridge, Massachusetts. Later the family moved to Cleveland, Ohio, and Beloit, Wisconsin. Henrietta had an uncle, Erasmus Leavitt, who lived in Cambridge, and when her father died he left an estate that included a nearby house. Eventually, Henrietta's mother moved back to Cambridge and lived with Henrietta.

Leavitt enrolled at Oberlin College in Ohio in 1885. In 1888 she transferred to the Society for the Collegiate Instruction of Women, in Cambridge, which later became Radcliffe College. In her last year as an undergraduate

---

1. Johnson, *Miss Leavitt's Stars*. Chapters 1–3 are mostly about Leavitt. Chapters 4–10 explain how astronomers used Leavitt's discovery to measure distances to stars.

she took her first astronomy course. In 1892, she graduated; that is, she was awarded a certificate testifying that she had done work deserving of a Harvard BA—if she had been a man.

After graduation, Leavitt began volunteering at the Harvard Observatory, doing stellar photometry and earning graduate credits. In 1896 she left for a two-year tour in Europe. Johnson notes that we don't know where she went or with whom.[2] Then she spent some years in Beloit, working as an art assistant at Beloit College and meeting "unexpected cares." We don't know if these "cares" had to do with her own health (in a letter she reported problems with her sight, and she was growing progressively deaf) or the health of family members (at various points in her career Leavitt interrupted her scientific work to nurse relatives). In 1902 she wrote to Edward Pickering at Harvard to ask if she could get back into astronomy. Since cold weather seemed to aggravate her hearing problem, could he recommend an observatory in a warm climate?[3] Pickering wrote that he didn't know of any warm-weather observatory that would want her, but he offered her a job as a "computer" at thirty cents an hour. Leavitt eagerly accepted, though her arrival in Cambridge was delayed by a relative's illness. Finally, in the fall of 1902, she had a paid position in astronomy. She worked for the Harvard Observatory for the rest of her life, with occasional interruptions caused by health problems of her relatives, her own illnesses (we know of at least one stomach surgery), and (more happily) vacations. She became head of the photometry department. In 1921, she died of cancer. Perhaps the best clues we have as to her personality and character are found in remarks written by Solon Bailey, a Harvard professor, in 1922:

> Miss Leavitt inherited, in a somewhat chastened form, the stern virtues of her puritan ancestors. She took life seriously. Her sense of duty, justice and loyalty was strong. For light amusements she appeared to care little. She was a devoted member of her intimate family circle, unselfishly considerate in her friendships, steadfastly loyal to her principles, and deeply conscientious and sincere in her attachment to her religion and church. She had the happy faculty of appreciating all that was worthy and lovable in others, and was possessed of a nature so full of sunshine that, to her, all of life became beautiful and full of meaning.[4]

2. Ibid., 30.

3. Ibid,, 31.

4. Ibid., 28.

5.2.2 The Standard Candle

Edward Pickering, head of the Harvard College Observatory from 1877 to 1919, found an innovative solution to a management problem. Pickering had great ambitions for the observatory. He wanted the observatory to lead the world in the use of new observational techniques—photography and spectrographic analysis. He wanted to create an exhaustive catalog of stars— not just their position but also their chemical makeup and luminosity. He wanted a precise method for comparing the luminosity of stars. He wanted lists of variable stars. And so on. Today we might call this basic research. Pickering wanted to find and organize data, lots of it, leaving it to other astronomers to use the information in support of theories. But in an age before government grants, the observatory's budget depended on patrons. He had to make every penny count. And in Pickering's day, all calculations had to be done by human beings.

Pickering's solution was to employ a new resource, which had just ar- rived in the scientific world: women. In the nineteenth century, the door to higher education for women had opened (a little) at institutions such as Oberlin College and the Society for the Collegiate Instruction of Women. Pickering found he could hire bright, college-educated women and pay them less than men. He made them "computers" for a standard wage of twenty-five cents an hour. (He offered Henrietta Leavitt thirty cents "in view of the quality of your work."[5]) Of course, he also hired men, and for the most part it was the men who managed the telescopes, both in Massachusetts and in Arequipa, Peru. The "computers" organized and analyzed data. Lest we be too harsh in our judgment of Pickering, we should note that none of his staff were highly paid; Johnson estimates that Pickering himself earned less than two dollars an hour.[6] And by hiring women, Pickering included them in cutting-edge research.

The observatory's telescopes were equipped with a clockwork mecha- nism that adjusted their aim to compensate for the earth's rotation; this allowed the astronomers to take long exposure photographs of the sky. Astrophotography vastly increased the reach of telescopes, revealing thou- sands of stars too dim to be detected before. The photographic negatives were glass plates. Pickering's team collected thousands of these plates; to this day they constitute a historical and scientific treasure trove, carefully preserved by the university.[7] Pickering assigned his computers the task of

5. Ibid., 32.

6. Ibid., 21.

7. Harvard is now engaged in digitizing the information on more than six hundred thousand historical astrographic plates. See Grindlay et al., "Digitizing the Harvard

examining, analyzing, and recording information from the astrographic plates. Much of Henrietta Leavitt's work took place standing at a desk on the second floor of an unremarkable university building, with a glass plate mounted on a small stand and backlit by mirrored light, meticulously measuring and recording the luminosity of stars.

On a glass negative, stars appear as black dots on a white field. When the pictures are developed, they appear as white dots on a black field. If the positive image is carefully aligned, sandwich style, with the negative, the whole field should be black. But if positive and negative images taken at different times are aligned, some stars peek through; they have become brighter in the interval. These "variable" stars change their luminosity. As early as 1784, an astronomer named John Goodricke (who, like Leavitt, was deaf) discovered that some variable stars brighten and fade in a consistent cycle; such stars are called Cepheids, after Delta Cephei, the first star Goodricke found with this characteristic.

So, in addition to recording the apparent brightness of stars, Pickering's computers were asked to compare positive and negative plates to discover variable stars. Leavitt proved exceptional at finding them. By 1904 she had found two hundred variables; in the next year she would find more than eight hundred variables. Charles Young of Princeton wrote to Pickering, "What a variable-star 'fiend' Miss Leavitt is. One can't keep up with the roll of new discoveries."[8] It is estimated that when she died Leavitt had discovered close to half of all variable stars known at the time.

As early as 1904 Leavitt had noticed something about Cepheids: it seemed that the brighter Cepheids had longer cycles. But since the distance to various stars differs greatly, how could one be sure that the apparent luminosity of a star represented its true luminosity? If the real luminosity of a Cepheid variable could be correlated to the period of its cycle, there might be a way to calculate the star's luminosity from its period. Leavitt continued to investigate the possible connection between period and luminosity as opportunity arose.

It is important to remember that Leavitt did not control her own research. She worked on whatever tasks Pickering assigned her. In 1907 he gave Leavitt an amazingly difficult job that would occupy most of her time for many years. Pickering had decided that modern astronomy needed a new, refined scale for stellar luminosity and that this scale should be based on astrophotography, because the camera recorded more of the light from a star than human eyes could see. The photometric scale would be based on

8. Young to Pickering, March 1, 1905. Quoted in Johnson, *Miss Leavitt's Stars*, 37.

forty-seven stars ranged around Polaris; these stars comprised the North Polar Sequence. Pickering wanted the Harvard North Polar Sequence to serve as a universal standard for stellar luminosity. Therefore, he wanted Leavitt to use all the relevant data available in calculating the relative brightness of all forty-seven stars—and that meant comparing plates from many different telescopes around the world. It was not merely a task of comparison; Leavitt had to be aware of the peculiar tendencies of each telescope and the spectrographic signature of each star. The image of a star on the edge of a photographic plate would be less accurate than one in the center. Her report on each star had to be based on careful examination of the plates, precise calculations, and sound argument.

While working on this enormous task, Leavitt continued to discover variable stars. Harvard astronomers in Peru had shipped hundreds of negatives of the Magellanic Clouds, an astronomical feature as familiar to people in the southern hemisphere as Polaris is to people in the north. In 1908 Leavitt published a twenty-one-page article in the *Annals of the Astronomical Observatory of Harvard College* titled "1777 Variables in the Magellanic Clouds."[9] Not surprisingly, most of the article was composed of tables listing the variable stars. But at the end of the article comes the kicker. Sixteen Cepheids had appeared on enough of the plates to work out their comparative magnitudes. Leavitt showed a list of them, giving the period of their cycles and their apparent magnitudes. Since all sixteen stars were in the Small Magellanic Cloud, for practical purposes they had the same distance from earth, which meant their apparent brightness corresponded to their actual brightness. Leavitt wrote, "It is worthy of notice that in Table VI the brighter variables have the longer periods."[10] The period of a Cepheid was a reliable clue as to its actual luminosity. How precise a clue?

Leavitt would continue to work on the topic, but not immediately. She fell ill and went to hospital. Then she returned to Wisconsin for convalescence. Pickering wanted her back at work on the North Polar Sequence, so we have an exchange of letters from 1909–1910 in which he inquired after her health and urged her to return. She apologized for her slow recovery and assured him of her enthusiasm for the work.[11] Pickering sent Leavitt some plates so she could resume her work while in Wisconsin. Finally, in the fall of 1910, she was back in Cambridge, working on the North Polar Sequence and variable stars in the Magellanic Clouds. The evidence in support of her idea became clear.

9. Leavitt, "1777 Variables in the Magellanic Clouds."
10. Ibid., 107.
11. Johnson, *Miss Leavitt's Stars*, 39–41.

In 1912, in *Harvard College Observatory Circular* 173, Pickering reported on the work of his assistant. "The following statement regarding the periods of 25 variable stars in the Small Magellanic Cloud has been prepared by Miss Leavitt." The "statement" turned out to be a groundbreaking article. In the article Leavitt convincingly showed that the period-luminosity (P-L) relationship was real. She wrote:

> A remarkable relation between the brightness of these variables and the length of their periods will be noticed. In H.A. 60, No. 4, attention was called to the fact that the brighter variables have the longer periods, but at that time it was felt that the number was too small to warrant the drawing of general conclusions. The periods of 8 additional variables which have been determined since that time, however, conform to the same law.[12]

Some authors have wondered whether Leavitt understood the importance of her discovery. History of science researcher Nick Allen thinks it is clear that she did. He cites as evidence the following quotations, also from Leavitt's groundbreaking article.

> They resemble the variables found in globular clusters, diminishing slowly in brightness, remaining near minimum for the greater part of the time, and increasing very rapidly to a brief maximum.[13]

And:

> Since the variables are probably at nearly the same distance from the Earth, their periods are apparently associated with their actual emission of light, as determined by their mass, density, and surface brightness.[14]

And:

> It is to be hoped, also, that the parallaxes of some variables of this type may be measured.[15]

And (in reference to a graph):

> A straight line can readily be drawn among each of the two series of points corresponding to maxima and minima, thus showing that there is a simple relation between the brightness

12. Leavitt, "Periods of 25 Variable Stars in the Small Magellanic Cloud," 1.
13. Ibid.
14. Ibid., 3.
15. Ibid.

of the variables and their periods. The logarithm of the period increases by about 0.48 for each increase of one magnitude in brightness.[16]

These quotes show (1) that Leavitt connected the P-L relationship to other important stellar characteristics; (2) that she recognized that if the distance to a few Cepheids could be determined by parallax then they would serve as astronomical milestones; and (3) that she also worked out the mathematical relationship between the length of period and the brightness of the star. It was as if she were telling the astronomical world: here's the cake; eat it.

It didn't take long for others to take the hint. In 1913 Ejnar Hertzsprung made the first attempt to calculate distances to thirteen Cepheids. There is no Cepheid close enough to Earth to measure the distance using an annual parallax, since the Earth's orbit is only two AU wide.[17] Once again stellar photography came to the rescue. The sun drags the Earth along as it moves through space—relative to the Local Standard of Rest, at about 2.8 AU per year.[18] So astrophotographs taken a few years apart gave Hertzsprung a long enough baseline to make his estimates. (I'm leaving out important statistical assumptions and details.) His result: the Small Magellanic Cloud was 30,000 light years away. Other astronomers followed, refined their assumptions and methods, and made corrections. Modern astronomers put the distance at 170,000 light years. But even Hertzsprung's conclusion showed that the universe is far larger than we had thought.[19]

Once astronomers were confident of the distance to a few Cepheids, Henrietta Leavitt's P-L relationship provided an easy way to determine other interstellar distances. The period of a Cepheid can be directly observed from Earth. The P-L relationship tells us what the star's real (as opposed to

16. Ibid., 2.

17. An Astronomical Unit (AU) is the distance from the earth to the Sun, roughly 93 million miles. Thus, if observations of a distant object are taken six months apart, the baseline of the observer's triangle is two AU. But the nearest star, Proxima Centauri, is about 268,000 AU away. Interstellar distances are usually measured in light years; one light year equals approximately 63,000 AU. In spite of the extreme acuteness of this triangle, it is possible to measure the distance to Proxima Centauri with an annual parallax. Other than a handful of nearby stars like Proxima Centauri, an annual parallax measurement becomes impossible.

18. The Local Standard of Rest is a point in space that moves around the center of the galaxy at the average speed of the stars in the local neighborhood. Although it is unnoticed by casual observers, the sun slowly changes its position relative to the "local" group of stars.

19. Hertzsprung's first publisher printed 3,000 rather than 30,000 light years, a typographical error that reflected the astronomical community's astonishment.

observed) luminosity is. Using Newton's inverse square law, a comparison of a star's real luminosity with its observed luminosity gives its distance. Astronomers call objects with known luminosity "standard candles," because they can be used in this way to measure distances.

Contemporary astronomers cross-check many different observations when establishing interstellar and intergalactic distances. But the P-L relationship of Cepheids makes them the easiest, most reliable standard candle.

In 1917 Henrietta Leavitt's work on the North Polar Sequence (which had expanded to ninety-six stars) was published in the *Annals of the Astronomical Observatory of Harvard College* (vol. 71, no. 3). It took up the entire issue—184 pages.[20] The scale of luminosity she created served as a standard reference tool for three decades.

At Harvard Observatory, Henrietta Leavitt was a "computer." She was head of photometry. But in 1920—a year and a half before she died—when the U.S. census taker came by and asked her occupation, she reported it as "astronomer."[21]

5.3 THE CASE OF ALFRED WEGENER

We know much more about Alfred Wegener's life and thought than we do about Henrietta Leavitt's. Besides his own books, letters, and journals, there are several biographies available, beginning with Else Wegener's books about her husband. The main source for this section is Roger M. McCoy's 2006 biography, *Ending in Ice*.

5.3.1 Wegener's Life

Alfred Wegener was born November 1, 1880, in Berlin, the youngest of five children born to Richard and Anna Wegener. Richard held a PhD in theology and classical languages and taught at a secondary school in Berlin. Alfred's academic interests were in science, not theology. He graduated from Friedrich Wilhelm University in 1902 with a degree in natural science, with an emphasis in astronomy. He worked as an astronomer in the Urania Society observatory while conducting research that led to a PhD in astronomy from the University of Berlin in 1905.

Almost immediately, Wegener turned his career focus away from astronomy. He was devoted to science, but he also wanted opportunities for

20. Johnson, *Miss Leavitt's Stars*, 57.
21. Ibid., 120.

travel and physical activity. He would have appreciated the importance of Henrietta Leavitt's discoveries, but we can speculate that Wegener would have been frustrated if confined to the sort of scientific work she did—the painstaking and patient comparison of photographic images taken by others.

Meteorology offered Wegener openings for adventure. In 1905 he took a job with his older brother, Kurt Wegener, a meteorologist, as an aide at the Aeronautic Observatory in Lindenburg. He learned to make meteorological measurements using kites and weather balloons. The brothers also took up recreational hot-air ballooning, and in 1906 they set a world record with a fifty-two hour flight.[22]

Also in 1906, as a vigorous twenty-six-year-old adventurer, Wegener was invited to join a Danish scientific expedition to Greenland led by Ludvig Mylius-Erichsen. Mylius-Erichsen wanted to study the Eskimos of Greenland, but he thought the expedition ought to collect data in many disciplines. Wegener was to serve as the expedition meteorologist. To prepare for the expedition, Wegener consulted with Wladimer Köppen, head of a meteorological kite station near Hamburg.

In Greenland, Wegener became the first person to collect high altitude polar climate data, using kites and balloons. For the first time, science began to get a picture of polar air circulation. He also learned, by harrowing experience, how dangerous arctic expeditions could be. Mylius-Erichsen and two others died when they ran out of food on a winter excursion. Nevertheless, Wegener and the rest of the expedition completed the planned two years of research. In 1908 Wegener returned to Germany, and in 1909 he became a *Privatdozent* at the University of Marburg. A *Privatdozent* doesn't hold a regular faculty position; Wegener's only pay came from the fees students paid to hear his lectures or from occasional honoraria. Wegener was a popular lecturer, but not having a regular faculty position brought him financial insecurity.

In 1911 Wegener published *The Thermodynamics of the Atmosphere* (*Thermodynamic der Atmosphäre*), which became a standard textbook for atmospheric physics. In spite of this success in his adopted discipline, his *Privatdozent* status required that he also lecture in astronomy.

After Wegener returned from Greenland, he became a regular visitor to the home of Wladimer Köppen, for two reasons. First, he and Köppen shared scientific ideas and encouraged each other's research interests. Second, Wegener fell in love with Köppen's daughter, Else. Alfred and Else married in 1913, after he returned from a second Greenland expedition in

---

22. McCoy, *Ending in Ice*, 9.

1912–13. On this expedition Wegener and three others narrowly escaped death when the glacier they were climbing suddenly calved. They also completed the longest trek across Greenland, 750 miles.

In 1914 World War I began, and Wegener, as a reserve army officer, was called into active duty. He was wounded in the shoulder, which allowed him to return home only three days after the birth of his daughter, Hilde. Many years later Else reflected on the strange implications of war: "How often he must suffer under the brutality of these mass murders. He is obligated to lead his men against the enemy, the 'enemy' with whom he recently, perhaps, engaged in an exchange of scientific ideas."[23] After a leave of two weeks, Wegener was back at the front; again he was wounded, this time in the neck, and his recuperation took several months.

In 1915 Wegener published *The Origin of Continents and Oceans* (*Die Entstehung der Kontinente und Ozeane*), which he finished while recovering from his injury. In this book Wegener argued for what he called "continental displacement" (which became known as "continental drift"), a theory that involved him in scientific controversy for the rest of his life.

Returning to active duty, Wegener served as a military meteorologist in various locations in Germany, Bulgaria, and Estonia. When possible, he used this time to pursue meteorological research. The year 1918 brought the end of the war, the birth of a daughter, Käthe, and Wegener's return to *Privatdozent* status at the University of Marburg. The family's fortunes were precarious at best. But when Wladimer Köppen retired, Wegener was hired as his replacement as head of the department of theoretical meteorology in the national weather service. The young family moved into the ground floor of the Köppens' house in Hamburg and the Köppens moved upstairs. This undoubtedly improved the financial situation for Wegener, but he still did not have a regular academic position. Besides his meteorological work, Wegener also gave occasional lectures at the newly established University of Hamburg. A third daughter, Charlotte, was born in 1920.

While in Hamburg, Wegener published a paper in which he argued that the craters of the moon are impact craters rather than volcanic calderas. While this idea was not entirely new at the time, Wegener may not have known about the previous literature.[24] Wegener's view eventually became widely accepted.

Finally, in 1924, the University of Graz, in Austria, offered Wegener a professorship. By this time Wegener's theory of continental displacement

---

23. Ibid., 12. Here McCoy quotes Else Wegener's 1960 compilation of her husband's writings, *Tagebücher, Briefe, Erinnerungen* (*Diaries, Letters, Memoirs*).

24. McCoy, *Ending in Ice*, 14. See McCoy's footnote discussion of lunar craters (179).

(or "drift") and the Greenland expeditions had made Wegener quite well known in German-speaking parts of Europe. One might think that universities would be eager to hire a scientist able to garner public enthusiasm. But Wegener was too controversial for most German universities.

After World War I, Germany suffered hyperinflation and extremely high unemployment. Economic reforms in 1924 brought some relief from inflation, but the overall economy remained weak. Wegener's hopes for another Greenland expedition had to be put on hold. But in 1928, the Emergency Aid Committee for German Science invited Wegener to propose such an expedition.[25] His proposal indicates the state of scientific knowledge of the polar regions in the 1920s as well as the breadth of Wegener's scientific interests. The expedition would consist of a preliminary exploration in 1929 and a full-year presence in 1930–31. Wegener planned to measure the thickness of the ice shelf by seismic means, measure interior elevations by altimeter, take gravity measurements, record ice temperatures at various depths in shafts, and take daily weather measurements at three locations (east coast, west coast, and in the center of Greenland) at 71° N. The meteorological data would be collected both at ground level and using weather balloons. Overall, the expedition could be expected to produce mountains of evidence about glacial and weather conditions in a large arctic area, information that would have almost immediate practical benefits to North Atlantic shipping, potential North Atlantic air travel (Lindbergh's 1927 flight had excited people on both sides of the Atlantic about transatlantic flight), and to European weather bureaus (because the Greenland air mass greatly influences European weather patterns).[26]

In 1929 Wegener, Johannes Georgi (who had taken part in the 1912 expedition), Fritz Loewe, and Ernst Sorge conducted the preliminary exploration on the west coast of Greenland. In the summer, the ice on the west coast of Greenland breaks up significantly earlier than the east coast ice, so the effort to establish a research station in the middle of the island, which would require transporting large amounts of matériel by multiple dogsled trips, had to be launched from the west coast. Wegener and his companions chose an embarkation point at the foot of the Kamarujuk glacier, which required the expedition to haul its supplies from sea level to an elevation of over 3,200 feet in a distance of 2.5 miles. In spite of the obvious difficulty of this location, other possibilities on the Greenland coast were even more forbidding, with steeper glaciers or dangers from glacier calving or more crevasses in the icefall. The preliminary expedition established the West

25. Ibid., 48.
26. Ibid.

Station and conducted the first seismic testing of the Greenland ice cap. Twenty-six miles inland from the coast they measured the ice at 3,651 feet thick. (Today we know that much further inland the ice cap is about 11,000 feet thick.)[27] Having achieved their preliminary goals, the expedition returned to Germany.

On April 1, 1930, the main expedition left Copenhagen. In Iceland they picked up twenty-five ponies and three Icelanders to care for the ponies and lead pack trains. Wegener's experiences in Greenland had convinced him that both ponies and sled dogs were useful in arctic exploration. He was also very excited about the use of a new invention—two motor-powered sleds with rear-mounted pushing propellers. If they worked properly, the powered sleds would greatly speed up matériel transport on the ice. Arctic exploration stood on the edge of a new age, the age of wide-track snow vehicles, instant radio communication, and life-saving airdrops and airlifts. In 1930, though Wegener anticipated such changes, exploration still depended on dogs, ponies, and manpower.

Once they arrived in Greenland, delays dogged the expedition. The sea ice in Umanak Fjord took several weeks longer to break up than expected, and packing the expedition's equipment up the glacier to West Station required several more weeks. The powered sleds had to be assembled and tested; this, too, took longer than expected, and the machines were prone to malfunctions due to cold, wind, deep snow, and heavy loads. In the end, the powered sleds accomplished very little actual matériel transport in 1930. By the following year, with more experience, the expedition was able to use them more effectively.

From the West Station, the expedition set out trail markers and established supply caches on the route to "Eismitte" (middle of the ice), Wegener's name for the central Greenland research station. The first dogsled trip to Eismitte, led by Georgi, did not leave West Station until July 15. In fifteen days they covered the 250-mile route, a route that climbed from a little over 3,000 feet to more than 9,000 feet, most of the time against the prevailing wind. However, in that time more than half of the Greenlanders hired to manage the dogsled teams had turned back; only Georgi, Karl Weiken, and three Greenlanders reached the Eismitte location—and with greatly reduced loads of matériel. On July 31, Weiken and the Greenlanders departed for the return to West Station. Going downhill, with the wind, and with much-reduced loads, the four made it to West Station relatively quickly. Johannes Georgi was left to establish the central research station alone.

27. Ibid., 55.

A second dogsled trip, led by Loewe, made it to Eismitte on August 18, and a third on September 13. Each trip increased the store of supplies at the central station, but never with as much as planned. The inherent difficulty of the journey, the health of the dogs, and the understandable reluctance of the Greenlanders to travel deep into the ice wilderness forced each sortie to cache supplies along the way. Georgi and Sorge, who were to stay the winter at Eismitte, sent a letter to Wegener with the third group when it returned to West Station. They calculated that their fuel supply would not last the winter. If a fourth supply trip did not reach them by October 20, they said they would set out for West Station on skis or snowshoes. Wegener had reached a similar conclusion about fuel, and he had been preparing a fourth supply trip before he read the letter on September 21. On September 22, the fourth trip, led by Wegener, started out. All of the difficulties faced by the earlier supply trips were encountered again—but this time they were greatly increased by the onset of colder weather. Wegener, Loewe, and one Greenlander named Rusmus Villumsen reached Eismitte on October 29. (The fifteen-day trek of the summer had become a thirty-five-day struggle in the fall.) Twelve other Greenlanders had turned back. Loewe suffered from serious frostbite. The fourth trip had to cache so much of their loads that they did not effectively increase the fuel stock at Eismitte at all.

In the interim, Georgi and Sorge had discovered how to minimize their fuel usage and still keep their ice station habitable (temperature maximum of 26° F—they couldn't risk melting the ceiling). Recalculating their fuel needs, they realized they could stay the winter, so they had abandoned their plan to snowshoe out, which everyone agreed was a counsel of desperation. But now three more men had arrived at Eismitte without improving their supply situation. Loewe, suffering from frozen toes on both feet, had to stay. Wegener and Villumsen decided to take two dogsled teams and head back to West Station. With a shortage of food, they expected the dogs to weaken; as they died, they would be cut up for food for the other dogs. Eventually, Wegener's sled would have to be abandoned and he would ski while Villumsen managed the last team of dogs.

Wegener and Rasmus Villumsen left Eismitte on November 1, venturing into an early winter with temperatures frequently as low as -50° F. They encountered almost perpetual darkness, high winds, and storms that prevented travel for days. They never reached West Station. On May 7, 1931, a team using a motor sled (repaired and now working properly) relieved the three men in Eismitte. Only at this time did the expedition members know with certainty that Wegener had died. There was no radio at Eismitte, no way to tell West Station of Wegener and Villumsen's departure. The scientists at West Station hoped that Wegener survived by staying at the central

station, while Georgi, Sorge, and Loewe hoped that Wegener and Villumsen
had reached the coast. Wegener's body was found carefully buried in the
snow between sleeping bags, and the location marked with his skis. He had
apparently died of heart failure. (Wegener was in excellent physical condition, but he was fifty years old and a smoker. Trying to keep up on skis with
a dogsled team would have been extremely strenuous.) Villumsen's body
was never found.

5.3.2 Continental Displacement

Scientists still do not appear to understand sufficiently that all
earth sciences must contribute evidence toward unveiling the
state of our planet in earlier times, and that the truth of the
matter can only be reached by combing all this evidence. . . . It is
only by combing the information furnished by all the earth sciences that we can hope to determine "truth" here, that is to say,
to find the picture that sets out all the known facts in the best
arrangement and that therefore has the highest degree of prob-
ability. Further, we have to be prepared always for the possibility
that each new discovery, no matter what science furnishes it,
may modify the conclusions we draw.[28]

The reader can see from the account of Wegener's life just given that it is a
story well worth telling, combining the excitement of cutting-edge scientific
data collection with adventure and tragedy in an arctic environment. But if
a curious person were to consult encyclopedia entries or google Wegener's
name on the Internet, she would probably find very little about Wegener's
astronomical writings, his meteorological research, or his Greenland expeditions. Instead, Wegener is most famous for a theory he contributed to
geology. This part of the story probably begins with Wegener's father-in-law.

Wladimer Köppen, the meteorologist, was interested in climate. In
1900, using a nineteenth-century vegetation map of the world, he con-
structed a classification scheme for the various climate zones of the planet.
By 1918 Köppen had incorporated rainfall and temperature criteria into his
system. Köppen's classification scheme and his famous wall map of world
climate (which appeared in 1928) are still used, with some modifications.[29]
In chapter 3, I noted that different scientific theories answer different sorts
of questions. A classificatory scheme like Köppen's is a good example of

28. Wegener, *Origins of Continents and Oceans.*
29. McCoy, *Ending in Ice*, 18.

an important theory that aims first to organize data rather than to provide causal explanations or predictions (though these latter goals are not completely absent).

Armed with a climate system based on the present, Köppen turned his attention to climates of the geologic past. Was the earth's climate significantly different in the past or essentially similar to current climate? Obviously, relevant evidence could be found in the location of fossils. For instance, the fossil plants found in coal beds show that coal is formed from dense vegetation in tropical or subtropical climates. The plants that became coal beds in northern latitudes, such as England, could not have grown there in today's climate. The climate of England had to have been very different at one time.

In the years between his first and second Greenland expeditions (1908–1912), Alfred Wegener was a frequent visitor to the Köppen home. Wegener and Köppen had many discussions of the latter's climate scheme and of questions of paleoclimatology, the study of past climates. As early as 1910 Wegener was considering a hypothesis that might account for much paleoclimatological data: the idea that the continents move.

In 1911, while browsing in the library of the University of Marburg (where he was a *Privatdozent*), Wegener found a scientific article listing fossils of identical species on both sides of the Atlantic Ocean.[30] Wegener began looking for more examples of identical or similar plants and animals separated by oceans. He found them—lots of them. At the time, scientists hypothesized that in the geologic past land bridges had connected distant continents. Such a land bridge, the Isthmus of Panama, currently connects North and South America, and a similar bridge connected Asia and Alaska about 20,000 years ago, when an ice age lowered the world's sea level 120 meters. So land bridges are real features of earth's geobiological history. But a great number of such land bridges would have had to exist to account for all of the fossil matches.

From the first publication of relatively accurate maps of the Atlantic Ocean in the seventeenth century, people have noted the seeming "fit" between the western coastline of Africa and the eastern coastline of South America. Abraham Ortelius, Francis Bacon, Antonio Snider-Pellegrini, Benjamin Franklin, and others speculated on the possibility that the continents had once been joined. Wegener went beyond speculation. He went looking for evidence.

Wegener first aired his continental displacement hypothesis at a meeting of a geological society in Frankfurt am Main and again a few nights

30. See the biography of Wegener furnished by the University of California Museum of Paleontology on its website: www.ucmp.berkeley.edu/history/wegener.html.

later in Marburg, in 1912. Between 1912 and 1915 he gathered evidence and refined his ideas, publishing *The Origin of Continents and Oceans* in 1915.

In 1910 an American geologist, Frank Taylor, proposed that Africa and South America had once been joined and that they had separated along the Mid-Atlantic Ridge, moving in opposite directions.[31] To that extent, his hypothesis sounds much like plate tectonic theory of today. He also speculated that mountain ranges were folded forward edges of moving continental landmasses, and that Antarctica was a leftover fragment of a supercontinent, from which other continents had separated.

Taylor and Wegener shared a crucial basic idea. Their theories were "mobilist"; the continents moved. Almost all geologists of the time were "fixists"; they assumed that the continents and oceans did not move laterally on the earth's surface. Taylor first presented an oral version of his 1910 paper in 1908. Later, some reviewers criticized Wegener for borrowing Taylor's idea and not crediting him. It is more likely that both men hit on the same idea independently, much as Leibniz and Newton invented (or discovered) calculus independently. It is clear that Taylor's paper consisted largely of speculation, while Wegener amassed a great deal of data in support of the idea.

First, there was the apparent "fit" of the continents, which can be seen on a map. And then seafloor mapping showed that the continental shelves fit even better. Second, Wegener pointed to many fossil examples of identical animals and plants on widely separated continents. He showed how, if the continents had been contiguous at one time, the distribution ranges of these species matched up. Third, continental displacement could explain paleoclimatic questions: how did coal deposits and other indications of tropical climates occur in temperate or arctic zones? (Answer: they had formed in tropical areas and later moved to their present locations.) Why did evidence of glaciers occur in rocks of the same age in widely separated parts of the world? (Answer: those parts of the world were close together long ago—and located where glaciers would form.) Fourth, the continental drift explained geologic formations. For instance, when Wegener pushed the continents together, the Appalachian Mountains lined up with mountains in Britain. The Zwartberg folded mountain range in South Africa lined up with the Sierras of South America.[32]

It is important to notice how Wegener drew on different sciences to support his theory. Nowadays, a scientist like Wegener is called "interdisciplinary," and we recognize that theoretical work drawing on evidence and

31. McCoy, *Ending in Ice*, 20.
32. Ibid., 24–26.

concepts from diverse fields can produce breakthroughs. But in the 1920s, Wegener's lack of qualifications in geology was a source of deep resistance. What authority does a meteorologist whose training was in astronomy and who dabbles in climatology have to instruct geologists?

Despite being unqualified in the eyes of many geologists, Wegener supported his theory with enough evidence that the idea had to be taken seriously. In the 1920s, two international conferences of professional geologists were organized, one in London and one in New York, to discuss the theory. Geologists who opposed Wegener's theory dominated both conferences. They attacked on several fronts.

First, what possible force could cause the continents to move laterally? Wegener had speculated that the gravity of the moon and centrifugal force, over a long period of time, might pull the continents along. The critics pointed out that the moon's pull was simply too weak for the job. Second, how fast did the continents move? Wegener used measurements of latitude and longitude made by explorers at various times in the nineteenth century to estimate that Greenland was moving away from Europe at a rate of approximately one hundred feet per year. But at that rate Greenland could circle the globe in several million years—something was clearly wrong! Third, how could continental landmasses, which are on average less dense than seabed rock, "plow through" that denser rock without breaking up? Wegener himself thought of the problem this way and did not have a convincing answer.

On all of these points, and more besides, the critics were right. Wegener's theory was wrong on important details, and this is a point worth remembering. But his critics drew the wrong conclusions from his errors. First, most of them seemed content to reason that since some of Wegener's supporting theses were wrong, the main thesis was also wrong. Second, they seemed to think that since Wegener had no professional qualifications in geology that his geological theory lacked strength.

The Dutch geologist who organized the New York meeting, W.A.J.M. van Waterschoot van der Gracht, warned his fellow geologists that they were missing the point. The basic question was "fixism" versus "mobilism," not the details of Wegener's mobilist theory. And van der Gracht thought that some form of continental drift (perhaps not Wegener's) would best answer the paleoclimatic questions Wegener had raised.[33] Essentially, he asked the geologic community to keep an open mind. They did not. "Continental drift" became the subject of derision among geologists for thirty years.

33. Ibid., 37.

Roger McCoy reports that, in the 1950s, graduate courses in geology treated Wegener's idea mostly as comic relief.[34]

Actually, Wegener's theory was resisted from the start. His first papers on the subject were strongly criticized in 1912, and Wladimer Köppen warned his son-in-law about the reception he would receive if he stepped outside of meteorology. But Wegener was committed to his idea. He continued to gather evidence before and after the publication of *The Origin of Continents and Oceans*. He published successive editions of the book in 1920, 1922, and 1929. In the third edition he introduced the term *Pangaea* (Greek: "all-earth") for the supercontinent from which the current continents broke apart. In the fourth edition, he noted that recent observations showed that shallower parts of the ocean had geologically younger seabeds, and he entertained the idea that the continental bodies might float on the rock below them. These hints have led some recent biographers to speculate that if Wegener had not died in 1930, he would have hit on solutions to many of the weaknesses in his theory. But that can only be speculation. What is clear is that in the face of almost universal rejection by geologists, Wegener believed that his theory was largely correct. Because of that belief, he continued to look for and find evidence to support his theory.

Earth science moved ahead on many fronts after World War II. In the 1950s, seafloor topography progressed to the point that the first comprehensive seafloor maps could be published. The vast extent of seafloor "rises"—really, mid-ocean mountain ranges—became evident. Worldwide seismographic data (collected partly to monitor nuclear weapons testing) revealed very definite earthquake zones arcing around the planet. And studies of the earth's magnetic field provided another stream of evidence.

Pierre Curie had shown that igneous rocks at a certain crucial temperature (the Curie point) adopt the magnetic polarity of the earth at that time and then retain it when they cool. Thus, igneous rocks serve as markers of the earth's polarity at the time they were hot. As early as 1929 a Japanese researcher, Motonari Matuyama, pointed out that the polarity of rocks younger than ten thousand years all line up with the earth's current magnetic field, while older rocks had all sorts of magnetic orientations, though his work was largely ignored in Europe and America.[35] The obvious explanation was that the earth's magnetic field had changed in the past. But had it "wandered" in many directions? In the 1950s new technology allowed scientists to record the magnetic orientation of seabed rocks, and the pattern became clear. On both sides of the mid-ocean mountain ranges, long strips

34. Ibid., 6.
35. Ibid., 152.

of parallel magnetism mirrored each other, with the newer strips nearer the mid-ocean rise and the older strips further away. (New rock under the shallow water and old rock under the deeper water, the clue Wegener noted in 1929.) As a result of this information, scientists quickly adopted the theory of "seafloor spreading." New rock rises from the earth's mantle in the mid-ocean rifts and spreads in opposite directions. Here was direct evidence of lateral movement in the earth's crust. Furthermore, the odd alignments of polarity in continental rock formations could be explained if the continents had moved.

Wegener's theory was not completely right. The continents do not plow through the denser rock of the seabed. Rather, the continents and the oceans alike rest on "plates." The theory of plate tectonics holds that the earth's lithospheric plates (the rigid crust and the uppermost layer of the mantle) float on the asthenosphere (the deeper, hotter, more fluid part of the upper mantle) below them. Lunar gravity has little to do with continental movement. Rather, plate tectonic theory holds that upwelling currents in the mantle create rifts between the plates. New rock forms at such rifts, and this pushes the plates apart. At their forward edges, the earth's plates can push into each other, causing mountain ranges (such as the Himalayas); or they can grind past each other (causing earthquakes on a fault line); or one can slide under another in a subduction zone (causing volcanic mountain ranges like the Cascades/Sierras). The earthquake zones mapped by seismologists since World War II roughly indicate the edges of the world's tectonic plates.

5.4 REFLECTIONS ON THE CASES

What can we conclude from just two examples? The cases of Henrietta Leavitt and Alfred Wegener do not by themselves constitute a representative sample of all scientists. But the reader probably knows of other examples— cases of actual scientific practice—that resemble the stories of Leavitt and Wegener in certain respects. The reader may then judge for herself: do these stories reflect common themes in science?

The point of the cases, remember, is to illustrate virtue. If it is true that faith helped Leavitt and Wegener to achieve scientific success, then insofar as these cases are representative of scientific practice the cases show that faith is a virtue.

Let's start with an obvious and easy point. Alfred Wegener believed in his theory of continental displacement and he was stubbornly "for" it, even in the face of personal attacks and opposition from experts. This perfectly matches the definition I offered for faith$_{(8)}$ in chapter 2. Wegener's faith in his theory helped him persist in looking for evidence in its favor. As a result, his work moved us toward a better *understanding* of paleoclimatology and geology. Since his faith helped him gain the internal goods of the practice of scientific research, Wegener counts as evidence for my thesis that faith is a MacIntyrean virtue.

But surely there are objections that ought to be raised. Someone might object: it turned out that Wegener's "mobilism" was right and the "fixists" were wrong. But isn't that an accident? We don't want to count his faith as a virtue just because he was lucky. Another way to put this objection is this: didn't Wegener's opponents among geologists also display faith? After all, they *believed* in their fixist theories and they were *for* them. But their faith was in error. Doesn't this show that on both sides faith was inappropriate? Neither mobilists nor fixists should have believed their theories; instead, they should have strictly governed their beliefs by the evidence. (It is easy to imagine the evidentialists objecting along these lines.)

In reply, I point out, first, that MacIntyre only says that virtues "tend" to help us achieve the internal goods of practices. A characteristic doesn't have to bear fruit every time to count as a virtue. Second, I suggest that the faith of the fixists could well have been a real virtue, helping move the geological community toward understanding, if it helpfully organized and motivated their research. Scientific investigations take time, energy, and cooperation; faith can help scientists pursue their work over the long haul, even when the propositional content of the faith is wrong.

Third, I think the objection rests partly on the erroneous idea that faith precludes further research. Remember Wegener's words quoted above: "we have to be prepared always for the possibility that each new discovery, no matter what science furnishes it, may modify the conclusions we draw." Clearly, Wegener believed in his theory—he stubbornly produced four editions of his book! But at the same time he recognized, and urged others to recognize, that one must be always open to new evidence, even if it turns out to be evidence from some other discipline.

These reflections raise the possibility that faith may be a MacIntyrean virtue even when the thing believed (a scientific theory, in this case) is false. I am not suggesting that the truth or falsity of the thing believed is immaterial to virtue. It is better to believe truth than error. But belief in and commitment to a theory (i.e., faith in a theory) may tend to help us gain understanding even when that theory proves deficient. Thus, it was phlogiston chemists of the eighteenth century who pursued research questions that eventually overturned belief in phlogiston.[36] We have to ask: does the faith in question sustain the believers in their quest for understanding? It is true that we can find in the history of science cases in which "faith" was nothing more than an alibi for closed-mindedness or jealousy, as in the celebrated Galileo case, in which the astronomer was forced to recant his scientific views because (some argued) those views contradicted the teaching of the church.[37] Galileo's opponents were closer to Pudd'nhead Wilson ("Faith is believing what you know ain't so"—faith$_{(1)}$) than to faith$_{(8)}$. As I said in chapter 3, a real virtue ought to be compatible with other relevant virtues, though I do not go so far as to say the virtues imply one another. A so-called faith that is incompatible with virtues such as attention to detail, open-mindedness, carefulness, and honesty (all virtues relevant to success in science) is not a real virtue. Wegener stubbornly believed in continental displacement, yet he combined that belief with great attention to detail, open-mindedness, and honesty.

Recall from chapter 2 the widespread notion that faith is opposed to doubt, with the result that a person with faith about some matter cannot have doubts about it, and vice versa (faith$_{(2)}$). This idea has sometimes been promoted as a Christian idea and linked to certain biblical texts. (For example, in Matthew 14:31 Jesus says to Peter, "You of little faith, why did you doubt?") I will not discuss religious faith now; I leave that topic for chapter 8. But it should be clear that nothing I have said so far in this book requires this notion. One can *believe* something and be *for* it while still having *doubts* about it. As I said in chapter 2, this is the *typical* case with faith$_{(8)}$. Doubts often will provoke the believer to explore the matter further. I think Wegener is a helpful example of a person with faith in a theory who at the same time searches for evidence to confirm that theory. Of course, the evidence may disconfirm the theory, even if the investigator doesn't expect it—and Wegener explicitly recognized this.

Other objections will focus on Henrietta Leavitt. How does Leavitt illustrate my thesis? Astronomers did not reject her period-luminosity theory the way geologists opposed Wegener; they latched onto Leavitt's discovery with enthusiasm, using it to drastically reshape our view of the universe in the 1920s. If faith means believing something that other people don't

36. In the seventeenth and eighteenth centuries, scientists hypothesized that combustible objects contained "phlogiston," an element that was realized in the process of burning. Phlogiston chemistry was overturned with the discovery of oxygen in the late eighteenth century.

37. The Galileo case is too often given a tendentious and simplistic interpretation: religion versus science. Galileo's chief opponents were Aristotelian scientists who manipulated the authority of the church to silence him.

believe, it doesn't seem to apply to the P-L theory. As soon as other astronomers read her work, they believed it.

Leavitt more clearly illustrates faith$_{(7)}$ than faith$_{(8)}$. She spent countless hours standing at a desk, carefully examining photographic plates from observatories all over the world. The plates of the Magellanic Clouds came from Peru. Her subsidiary attention *indwelt* these bits of black and white on glass plates. Her focal attention stretched into interstellar distances in a search for understanding. As Polanyi pointed out, one mark of reality is that contact with it provokes further questions; as soon as Leavitt published her P-L discovery, a whole new era in astronomy began. Within ten years of Leavitt's death human beings had learned that there were galaxies other than our own and that they are all moving away from us.

But I think there may be overlap between my examples. I remind the reader that we are tempted to overinterpret the little we know about Henrietta Leavitt. Nevertheless, I will take that risk.

Henrietta Leavitt was a *woman* who was *deaf*. She was hired to be a *computer*. But she reported herself to be an *astronomer*. I think it is reasonable to infer that she held certain beliefs and that she acted on those beliefs. If so, she is an example of faith$_{(8)}$ as well as faith$_{(7)}$. And that faith$_{(8)}$ sustained her in scientific work that led to significant increases in understanding.

What was it that she believed? We don't know, and I can only offer conjectures. I suspect that she believed that women could do scientific work equal to men's. She may have believed that deafness was a physical handicap that in no way limited her ability to observe, record, and analyze information. Needless to say, in Leavitt's lifetime, there were people who would have denied both notions.

At some point she undoubtedly came to believe that the brighter Cepheids had longer periods—sometime after her initial observation in 1904 but probably well before her 1912 "statement." I suspect she believed that, though Pickering controlled her research assignments, the work she put in on variable stars was worthwhile.

I don't suppose such conjectures are perfectly accurate. But it seems very unlikely that Leavitt could have done what she did without some beliefs along these lines.

Leavitt's case illustrates faith$_{(8)}$ in a different way than does Wegener's story. Her faith, if my conjectures are close to the truth, was not so much in her scientific idea (though she did pursue it for years, while primarily engaged in the North Polar Sequence) as in herself and her work. I noted in chapter 3 that parents sometimes find it hard to express what they believe as a proposition; they are working for something that they may not be able to name. Leavitt's case might be similar. Psychologically, it seems necessary that she *believed*—this work is worth doing; I, a woman, can do this work; in spite of deafness and other health problems, I can do this; and so on.

Neither Leavitt nor Wegener lived by faith alone. Clearly, each of them displayed many virtues relevant to their scientific success. They displayed persistence, attention to detail, curiosity, and honesty. Leavitt's work involved a level of meticulousness hard to imagine in a day of electronic calculators. One could argue that even Wegener's physical courage and sense of adventure contributed to his scientific success.

The point here is one MacIntyre would welcome. Virtues are virtues in relation to practices, and practices are complex social activities; therefore we should expect that success in practices will require constellations of virtues, not just faith alone. And, given the various kinds of faith listed in chapter 2, success in practices may require more than one kind of faith.

By pointing to Wegener and Leavitt as examples of virtue, I do not imply that they are examples of perfection. Wegener eagerly recognized the potential of motorized transport for arctic exploration. As things turned out, radio communication could have prevented a tragedy; why didn't he see the potential there? Did his penchant for adventure contribute to his death? Someone might criticize Wegener for a deficiency of prudence. But we don't need perfect examples. On Aristotle's advice, all we need are human examples of virtue whom we can recognize and imitate. If we admire and study multiple exemplars, we can imitate their virtues rather than their vices.

6

Faith as a Virtue in Social and Political Reform

In this chapter I turn to examples in which faith sustains persons engaged in social and political reform. People who challenge the status quo almost invariably face resistance, and the more radical the changes sought the stronger the resistance. Often reformers must overcome violence, libel and slander, intimidation, defeats, and the unfaithfulness of allies. That reformers need faith may seem obvious; in terms of supporting the main argument of the book, given in chapter 3, the reader might wonder whether these examples are needed. They are.

I hope not only to argue that faith is a virtue but also to help the reader (and myself) better understand this virtue and grow into it. By comparing and contrasting exemplars we may get a better grasp of what is central to virtue and what belongs to the periphery. Perhaps the value of this chapter is not so much in advancing the argument of chapter 3 as in pointing to examples we might emulate.

6.1 THE CASE OF WILLIAM WILBERFORCE

A 2006 movie, *Amazing Grace*, and Eric Metaxas' best-selling book of the same title have brought the name of William Wilberforce to the attention of a popular audience, particularly in the United States, thus rescuing him (for a while anyway) from historical obscurity. To most people in America or Britain Wilberforce is no more familiar than Martin van Buren or William

Grenville (respectively: U.S. president and British prime minister in the early 1800s). In his time, though, William Wilberforce was famous throughout Britain, and in 1856 Wilberforce University, in Ohio, was founded in his honor; later it became the first college owned and operated by African Americans.[1] When Wilberforce died, he was buried in Westminster Abbey, and his pallbearers included the speaker, the lord chancellor, two dukes and four peers of the realm.[2] He was, as the newspapers repeated, "the conscience of the nation." In New York and Jamaica, people of African descent went into mourning.

6.1.1 Wilberforce's Life

William Wilberforce was born to a wealthy merchant family in Hull, England, on August 24, 1759. His grandfather, also named William, changed the family name from Wilberfoss ("foss" means "servant") to Wilberforce. This grandfather built up the family fortune (Baltic trade and shipping) and became a major player in Yorkshire politics; he was twice elected Mayor of Hull. His second son, Robert, took over the family business in 1755, and became the father of our William Wilberforce. The grandfather's first son (another William) had left the family business behind, moving to London and marrying Hannah Thornton, whose father was a member of Parliament and director of the Bank of England.

Young William's cozy childhood was shaken by sickness. First his older sister died, followed by his father, and then his mother fell seriously ill. At ten years old, William was sent to live with his uncle and aunt, William and Hannah Wilberforce. This couple was childless (which probably explains why second son Robert named his son William), extremely wealthy, and deeply committed to a new popular movement in English religion: evangelicalism.

Though orthodox in all their creedal positions, evangelical preachers like George Whitefield and John and Charles Wesley brought a new vibrancy to Christianity in England and America. They preached to the poor and to huge open-air crowds. (Skeptical of numbers he had heard, Benjamin Franklin attended one of Whitefield's sermons in America. He walked around the gathered audience and estimated the number of people to be twenty thousand.[3]) Evangelical preachers managed to combine an emphasis

1. The university is still very much a going concern, in many ways an honor to its namesake. See the university website: www.wilberforce.edu.

2. Metaxas, *Amazing Grace*, 276.

3. Ibid., 9.

on God's grace to sinners, an insistence on personal and social rectitude, and, at least in the Wesleys' case, a belief that political and social circumstances can be changed. The current social order may not be the result of God's will; in fact, God wills that Christians work to oppose injustice.[4] In the home of William and Hannah Wilberforce, young William Wilberforce was introduced to evangelical Christianity, with its emphasis on personal rectitude and concern for poor people, for native peoples in the empire, and for Africans.

Few among England's upper class had sympathy for evangelicals' moral strictures or their friendliness with the underclass. Wilberforce's mother and grandfather had no desire that he be a Methodist. When they discovered their mistake, they removed the twelve-year-old William from William and Hannah's home. Back in Hull, after a few years, young William abandoned the seriousness of his aunt and uncle and joined enthusiastically into the round of dances, plays, parties, and amusements of England's wealthy class. Grandfather William and uncle William both died in 1776, making our William very wealthy indeed; in the same year he entered Cambridge, where he spent most of his time partying.

Wilberforce was a short (just over five feet tall), slight man who often suffered digestive ailments. Modern biographers suggest he had ulcerative colitis. For much of his life, he took regulated doses of opium to control pain. Gradually, this drug use made his poor eyesight worse. When sick, his weight could drop below one hundred pounds. Nevertheless, people who knew him said he had a marvelous speaking and singing voice, an agile mind, and a lively sense of humor. He was the life of the party.

In 1779–80, Wilberforce began attending sessions of Parliament, where he deepened his friendship with William Pitt, a fellow Cambridge student and son of the former prime minister. Pitt's family connections destined him for politics; Wilberforce decided to enter politics too. He had no particular political cause or interest, but he was wealthy, witty, skillful in debate, and ambitious. In 1780, at the age of twenty-one, Wilberforce spent liberally and won election as M.P. from Hull.

In the early 1780s, Wilberforce had arrived, so to speak. He was young, single, rich, a member of five private clubs (where he gambled and gained notoriety for his wit and singing voice), and a close friend of William Pitt, the rising star of British politics. In 1783, with the fall of a coalition in Parliament, the king asked Pitt to form a new government—which would make Pitt, at twenty-four, the prime minister! The new government was politically weak, and it surprised no one that Pitt had to dissolve Parliament and call for

---

4. Brendlinger, *Social Justice Through the Eyes of Wesley*, 160–61.

an election in the spring of 1784. Wilberforce decided to stand for election in York—a traditionally important seat, with twenty times the population of Hull—and in a remarkable upset he won, contributing to a nationwide triumph that strengthened Pitt's government.[5]

In 1784–85 Wilberforce was converted to evangelicalism, largely through the influence of Isaac Milner, a brilliant son of a weaver who was later to hold the Lucasian chair in mathematics and chemistry at Cambridge. While he remained a member of the Church of England, his conversion turned his religion into a matter of deep personal conviction rather than a collection of occasional public rituals, the superficial civil religion practiced by much of the upper class. As a consequence of his conversion, he resigned his memberships in the five social clubs. He wrote a letter to Pitt, saying that he might need to resign from Parliament, because he had to give service to God primacy in his life. In response, Pitt asked Wilberforce to do nothing rashly. God gave men all sorts of work to do on earth; could not God's plan for Wilberforce include political service? Wilberforce took his worries to John Newton, an evangelical minister and author of popular hymns (including "Amazing Grace"). To his surprise, Newton's advice mirrored Pitt's: Wilberforce should serve God in Parliament.[6]

To what use should Wilberforce put his position of influence? In 1786–87 Wilberforce gradually came to the conclusion that he should devote his life to "two great objects: the suppression of the Slave Trade and the reformation of manners."[7] By "reformation of manners" he meant moral reform. In chapter 3 I pointed out that some social and political reformers aim at improving the moral climate of society; Wilberforce was one of them. To a large degree, the "reformation of manners" was nonpolitical; Wilberforce supported or took a leading role in societies devoted to helping North American Indians, Haitians, and victims of the Napoleonic wars. He also helped a group that worked to improve conditions in India, another that founded and sustained a colony of ex-slaves in Sierra Leone, and others that combated public drunkenness and aided children trapped in child labor (such as chimney sweeps).[8] But sometimes the "reformation of manners" called for new laws. For instance, Wilberforce moved to abolish public executions, bear and bull baiting, and the selling of the bodies of hanged

5. Metaxas, *Amazing Grace*, 35–40.

6. Fendall, *To Live Free*, 83–90.

7. Metaxas, *Amazing Grace*, 69.

8. Fendall, *To Live Free*, 126–27, 144.

criminals for dissection.[9] I will discuss the other "great object," the attack on the slave trade, below.

When he was thirty-seven years old, Wilberforce published a book with a long and explicit title: *A Practical View of the Prevailing Religious System of Professed Christians, in the Higher and Middle Classes in This Country, Contrasted with Real Christianity.* This book, the product of several years' reflection on his evangelical beliefs, sold surprisingly well, going through fifteen printings in England and twenty-five in America during Wilberforce's lifetime.[10] Perhaps the fact that the author was a nationally known politician rather than a priest or minister added to its cachet.

A Practical View came out on April 12, 1797, the Wednesday before Easter. But Wilberforce gave the event almost no attention in his journal—he was in the middle of a whirlwind romance.[11] He had recently confessed to a friend, Thomas Babington, that he no longer believed that he should always remain single. On Thursday Wilberforce's journal says that Babington urged him to consider marrying Barbara Spooner, a twenty-year-old evangelical who supported many of Wilberforce's political positions. On Holy Saturday, Wilberforce and Miss Spooner were introduced at a dinner. On Easter Sunday, Wilberforce's journal notes that his thoughts during worship were largely occupied by Miss Spooner and that he was in love. Within a week they were engaged, and six weeks later married. In spite of Wilberforce's recurring bad health, the marriage lasted thirty-five years and produced six children—and, from all accounts, much happiness.

In 1812, Wilberforce retreated from his highly demanding York seat to a "pocket borough" representing Bramber. He and Pitt both supported election reform in England, one aim of which was to eliminate such undemocratic boroughs, so his switch from York to Bramber compromised one of his political principles.[12] But it allowed Wilberforce to concentrate his dwindling energies on legislation rather than his service to constituents. He retired from Parliament in 1825.

Near the end of his life, Wilberforce's fortune ran out—for decades he had given generously to charitable causes of many sorts, and around 1830 he invested much of his remaining wealth in a dairy venture run by his oldest son, William. The dairy was a failure, and the younger William fled his debts, moving to the continent. Wilberforce sold his house and lands to

---

9. Metaxas, *Amazing Grace*, 74–77.

10. Fendall, *To Live Free*, 195.

11. Metaxas, *Amazing Grace*, 172–77.

12. Fendall, *To Live Free*, 225.

pay his son's debts.[13] During his last years, he and Barbara lived with their son Robert's family. Wilberforce refused to complain about his reduced circumstances; rather, he appreciated the opportunity to spend time with grandchildren. He died in 1833.

6.1.2 The Campaign against Slavery

The evangelical Christianity Wilberforce embraced holds that God loves all human beings.[14] Every person is a sinner, in need of divine grace, and God extends the opportunity of salvation to all. For evangelical preachers like John Wesley, these "religious" beliefs had social implications. From a theological perspective they could endorse what an Enlightenment thinker such as Thomas Jefferson labeled "self-evident" truths: all men are created equal and have natural rights. Wesley and Wilberforce did not think they had to produce biblical proof-texts against slavery; instead, they had only to point to the actual practice of slavery to show that it was inconsistent with belief in human equality, divine mercy, and the biblical command to love one's neighbor.[15]

After Pitt and Newton convinced Wilberforce to continue in Parliament, in 1786–87 he searched for a direction for his political career. In his childhood, while living with his Uncle William and Aunt Hannah, he had heard reports of the evils of the slave trade. In his year of searching, Wilberforce came into contact with several persons who pulled him into the abolitionist camp: the musician and self-taught lawyer Granville Sharp; Sir Charles Middleton, who later became comptroller of the navy, and his wife, Margaret; Olaudah Equiano, a freed slave; Reverend James Ramsey, who had seen conditions on slave ships and served a parish in St. Kitts in the West Indies; and a young clergyman, Thomas Clarkson, who wrote a prize-winning essay against slavery while still a student. John Newton himself was a retired sea captain who had experienced the slave trade firsthand and had later denounced it.[16] The abolitionist movement included Quakers and other nonconformists as well as evangelicals within the Church of England.

---

13. Ibid., 238.

14. Historically, there have been Christian denominations that deny that God loves every person. Some Protestant reformers held that God loves only those people whom he has chosen (or "elected") for salvation. The evangelicalism of eighteenth-century England was deeply influenced by John Wesley's more inclusive view of God's love.

15. Brendlinger, *Social Justice Through the Eyes of Wesley*, 54–55.

16. Metaxas, *Amazing Grace*, 91.

In 1787 Wilberforce became the Parliamentary leader of the anti-slavery movement. Before this time, the abolitionists had already won some ground. Granville Sharp had litigated the cases of Africans in England, winning a judgment against slavery on English soil. Ramsey and Clarkson published well-researched popular essays describing the horrible conditions on slave ships and on plantations in the West Indies. Equiano published a firsthand account of his experience of being enslaved. As time went on, the abolitionists pioneered tactics that would be used by other reform movements in democracies: they sought to change public consciousness through publishing; they circulated handbills depicting the crowded conditions on slave ships; they gathered signatures on petitions in every part of the country; they organized boycotts of sugar, because it was produced by slave labor; and they popularized what was perhaps the first political logo, Josiah Wedgwood's cameo image of an African in chains with the words, "Am I not a man and a brother?"

Also in 1787 Wilberforce first introduced his bill to abolish the slave trade. Parliament ordered an inquiry into the question, and the abolitionists were ready. They testified how slaves were usually procured in wars stirred up by Europeans among African tribes. They demonstrated the impossibly overcrowded conditions on slave ships. They reported how slaves were beaten, flogged, and tortured. They detailed the horrendous death tolls in the Atlantic crossing (and not only among the human cargo; as many as a quarter of the sailors on slave ships, pressed into service and little more than slaves themselves, died every year). They submitted firsthand reports of how slaves were worked to death in the West Indies. And they presented petitions with the signatures of thousands of Englishmen supporting the bill.[17]

Against all this, the anti-abolition forces resorted to the oldest of all political weapons: lies. They claimed that Africans were happy to be liberated from their savage lives in Africa, that Africans received humane (and expensive) treatment aboard ship, and that in the West Indies, slaves were civilized by being converted to Christianity and being taught to perform modern labor.[18]

Proslavery members of Parliament also argued that restriction of the slave trade would damage Britain's economy. If Britain left the trade, the profits would simply go to France. And Parliament needed more time to gather evidence and consider the matter. In spite of Wilberforce's eloquent plea for immediate action, the bill was tabled.

17. Ibid., 129–33.
18. Ibid., 134–35.

Wilberforce introduced bills against the slave trade repeatedly. He arranged for a select committee to hear testimony about the tabled bill so that he could question witnesses personally. The abolition movement continued to produce petitions and evidence. But revolution in France in 1789 turned the mood in Parliament against anything close to "republican" policies. In 1791, after a supreme effort by Wilberforce, the bill to suppress the slave trade came to a vote and lost 163–88. Popular support for abolition continued to grow, but to conservative minds that only made abolition more dangerous, more like the madness in Paris. In 1792 Parliament did pass a bill to abolish the slave trade—but only after inserting the word *gradually* into the bill, delaying implementation until 1796.

Then came war between Britain and the new French republic. In 1793 Parliament refused to confirm the vote for gradual abolition in 1796. Defenses of "liberty" and appeals to "human rights" now sounded unpatriotic to British parliamentarians. Wilberforce endured personal attacks and threats of violence. He was challenged to a duel, which he refused since he opposed dueling on moral grounds, but the matter added charges of cowardice to attacks on his character.[19]

In 1796 the prospect of success in Parliament seemed brighter. Wilberforce introduced yet another abolition bill, and it escaped the usual motion to table and passed first and second readings by narrow margins. But on the night of the final vote on the bill, a new Italian opera opened in London. Several MPs whose votes Wilberforce had counted on attended the opera and so missed the vote. The proslavery forces won by a slim margin, 74–70.[20]

As the struggle against the slave trade wore on, some prominent abolitionists died, and others, such as Clarkson, stepped aside in discouragement. From 1797 to 1807, Wilberforce continued to introduce abolitionist bills. In the early 1800s, he had very little parliamentary support. But by 1806 public opinion had settled against the slave trade and support in Parliament had grown, partly because the Act of Union in 1801 had brought pro-abolition Irish MPs into Parliament. Britain was now at war with Napoleon, and since the French emperor supported the slave trade, British politicians could support Wilberforce without appearing sympathetic to France. In 1806 William Pitt, worn out by the stress of leading an empire at war, died. William Grenville, a strong supporter of abolition, succeeded him as prime minister. In 1807 Grenville, a member of the House of Lords, introduced a bill against the slave trade and guided it to passage in the more conservative house, thus removing a difficulty that often plagued Wilberforce. On February 23, the

19. Ibid., 155–58.
20. Ibid., 164.

bill passed its third reading in the House of Commons. Wilberforce's first "great object" had taken twenty years to accomplish.[21]

Wilberforce went to work to secure legislation to enforce the new law against the slave trade, and later he moved to abolish slavery itself in the British Empire. He also supported Catholic emancipation. These issues outlasted Wilberforce's political career. Wilberforce retired from Parliament in 1825, and the bill to abolish slavery did not pass Parliament until 1833. Wilberforce was informed of victory in the House of Commons on July 27, two days before his death.

6.2 THE CASE OF DOROTHY DAY

In 2000, Cardinal John O'Connor of New York wrote to the Vatican proposing that Dorothy Day be recognized as a saint. Vatican officials approved the beginning of an investigation into her case. If her cause is successful, the process will undoubtedly take many years. She is currently recognized as "venerable." Perhaps it is ironic that while Dorothy Day still lived, she often discouraged any attempt to think of her as particularly holy: "Don't call me a saint. I don't want to be dismissed that easily."

In sharp contrast to the case of Henrietta Leavitt, we have extensive information about Dorothy Day's interior life. Day wrote several books, including a 1952 autobiography, gave countless interviews, and wrote columns or editorials for every issue of the *Catholic Worker* for over forty-five years. Readers who wish to learn more about her can consult the Catholic Worker website for links and references to this abundant literature.[22]

6.2.1 Day's Life before 1933

Dorothy Day was a journalist like her father and two older brothers—which only shows how little a career label like "journalist" really tells us about a person. Her father, John Day, was a sportswriter who covered horse racing and could be described as middle-class and patriotic. He disliked "trashy" dime-store novels, foreigners, blacks, and radicals. The older brothers, Donald and Sam, were conservative like their father; Sam later became managing editor of the *New York Journal American*.[23] In contrast, Dorothy, the third child of the family, began calling herself a socialist while a teenager,

---

21. Ibid., 208.

22. http://www.catholicworker.org/dorothyday/index.

23. Coles, *Dorothy Day*, 1.

and at nineteen she was writing for a socialist paper, *The Call*. As an adult she was attracted to the Catholic Church partly because it seemed to be the church that most welcomed immigrants.

In 1904 John Day moved his young family—he and his wife, Grace Satterlee Day, would have five children in all—to San Francisco. Dorothy was eight years old at the time of the San Francisco earthquake in 1906, which destroyed the newspaper where John Day worked. Unable to find newspaper work, John Day moved the family to Chicago, where he worked on a novel that was never published. By fierce economizing, Grace Day made a home for her children in spite of their poverty, and Dorothy's exposure to poverty on the south side of Chicago made a lasting impression on her. After two years John Day got a job with a Chicago newspaper, *The Inter Ocean*, which allowed the family to move to the north side of the city.

In 1914 Dorothy graduated high school and entered the University of Illinois at Urbana. She was an indifferent student, far more interested in politics and friendships than coursework. Dorothy read Jack London and Upton Sinclair and came to admire radical leaders like Eugene Debs. She befriended and roomed with Rayna Simons, a daughter of a wealthy Jewish family, who later became a communist and pursued revolutionary causes in China and Russia. Rayna died in Moscow in 1927, at the time of Dorothy's move into the Catholic Church. Their diverging beliefs did not keep Dorothy from regarding Rayna with respect and affection.[24]

John Day took a job with the *New York Morning Telegraph* in 1916. Dorothy's relationship with her father was strained at best, but she moved to New York to be closer to her mother, her sister Della, and her younger brother, John. Dorothy later would spend time in Europe, Mexico, New Orleans, and Chicago, but for most of her life New York remained home.

Dorothy had no desire to finish college. She plunged into what she later called a time of searching. She worked for two socialist newspapers, *The Call* and *The Masses*, writing stories about poor people, unemployed workers, anti-war and anti-conscription movements, and the campaign for women's suffrage. Sometimes she took part in the social movements she reported on; for instance, in between working for *The Call* and *The Masses*, she joined the Anti-Conscription League.[25] Invited by a friend, Peggy Baird, Dorothy joined a group of suffragettes who visited Washington, DC, to protest at the White House in 1917. Arrested and jailed, the women went on a hunger

---

24. Day, *Long Loneliness*, 70–71.
25. Forrest, *Love Is the Measure*, 24.

strike; on the tenth day they were freed by President Wilson's pardon.[26] It would be the first of many jail experiences for Dorothy Day.

In her time of searching, Dorothy went through several romantic and sexual relationships. In 1918 she took training as a nurse, thinking that as a nurse she could provide more immediate service to suffering people than a writer could. She fell in love with a handsome orderly at King's County Hospital named Lionel Moise. Moise was eight years older, a well-traveled adventurer who later became a journalist. He frankly told Dorothy he would not marry her; she ought to find someone else. Nevertheless, Dorothy pursued him and took no precautions; she became pregnant; and when Moise left to take a job in South America, she had an abortion.[27] A few months later, she married a much older man, Berkeley Tobey, "on the rebound," as she said. Tobey took her to Europe, where she drank heavily and wrote *The Eleventh Virgin*, a thinly fictionalized account of her affair with Moise. In 1921 she left Tobey and moved to Chicago, pursuing Moise. While in Chicago she had another experience in jail as a result of a federal raid on radicals, though the charge brought against her was being a "resident of a disorderly house," that is, a prostitute.[28] It was a brutal experience, one for which she later became thankful, as it brought home to her the suffering of prisoners. Only gradually, in 1922–23, did Dorothy break free of her obsession with Moise. She moved to New Orleans with a friend, Mary Gordon, for a year. By 1924 she was back in New York.[29]

Dorothy fell in love again, this time with Forster Batterham—a biologist, an atheist, and an anarchist. A Hollywood studio had purchased the film rights to *The Eleventh Virgin* (though no movie was made) for $5,000. With some of this money, Dorothy bought a small beach house on Staten Island where she could write. On weekends, Forster lived with her in the cottage. Forster loved the natural world; he shared many of Dorothy's concerns for social justice; and he thoroughly rejected compromise with institutions of state or church. Though never institutionally married, Dorothy referred to him as her common-law husband to the end of her life.[30]

At many points in her life, Dorothy had felt drawn to religion, especially to the Catholic Church. Her parents had married in an Episcopal church, though they didn't attend. In Chicago an Episcopal priest persuaded Grace Day to send her children to church, and Dorothy felt the beauty of

26. Ibid., 27–29.

27. Ibid., 35–37.

28. Ibid., 39.

29. Ibid., 38–40.

30. Ibid., 146.

the psalms and collects. Once, while looking for a friend named Kathryn, she came upon a Catholic neighbor, Mrs. Barrett, kneeling in prayer: "She turned to tell me that Kathryn and the children had all gone to the store and then went on with her praying. I felt a burst of love toward Mrs. Barrett that I have never forgotten."[31] While a university student, Dorothy consciously and deliberately turned away from religious faith, since the churches seemed to have little concern for the poor.[32] In her years of searching, Dorothy occasionally visited Catholic churches, finding them oases of peace in her confusing life. In the 1920s, while she mixed with New York literary and political figures such as Hart Crane, Allen Tate, Caroline Gordon, Malcolm Cowley, John Dos Passos, Eugene O'Neill, Mike Gold, and Kenneth Burke, she also continued to visit churches.[33] Her radical friends tended to criticize her interest in religion, but the attraction continued.

Dorothy became pregnant and gave birth to a daughter in 1927. Though he thought it wrong to bring children into a modern, unjust world, Forster Batterham did not shirk the responsibilities of fatherhood. He clearly loved Dorothy and their daughter. But Dorothy had Tamar baptized as a Catholic, something Forster regarded as superstitious nonsense. Dorothy began taking instruction to join the church herself. This forced a crisis, since Dorothy could not become a Catholic while living with Forster outside of marriage. Forster stuck to his anti-institutional principles; he would not marry. "Forster, the inarticulate, became garrulous only in wrath," Day reveals. "And his wrath, he said, was caused by my absorption in the supernatural rather than the natural, the unseen rather than the seen."[34] In December 1927, after yet another shouting match and separation, Dorothy denied Forster entrance to the beach house. On December 28, she was baptized.[35]

Dorothy later described her years with Forster as a time of "natural happiness." She wrote an article for *The New Masses* describing her joy in motherhood.[36] She was drawn to the Catholic Church as a place to express her gratitude. In her autobiography she explained that natural happiness was pulling her toward supernatural happiness. Her searching had led to genuinely good things: love shared with a good man and the delight of

---

31. Day, *Long Loneliness*, 25.
32. Ibid., 39–43.
33. Coles, *Dorothy Day*, 8.
34. Day, *Long Loneliness*, 120.
35. Forrest, *Love Is the Measure*, 49–51.
36. Coles, *Dorothy Day*, 9.

parenthood. But neither of these natural goods provided a final answer to her search.[37]

For five years after her conversion, Dorothy tried her hand at a variety of jobs, looking for some way to support herself and her daughter while integrating her social concerns with her religious faith. She summarized novels for MGM and for a short time in 1929 she moved to Hollywood to work for Pathé Motion Picture Company. She worked part-time for the Fellowship of Reconciliation, and one summer she cooked for Catholic seminarians. In 1930, she moved to Mexico City, where she felt encouragement, living amongst a majority Catholic population. But Tamar contracted malaria, so they returned to New York.[38] She continued writing—another autobiographical novel (unpublished), a gardening column for a Staten Island newspaper, and occasional articles for Catholic magazines. In December 1932, as the Great Depression worsened, she traveled to Washington as a reporter for *Commonweal* and *America* to cover the Hunger March. This event, organized by communists, brought hundreds of marchers from New York to Washington to dramatize calls for jobs, unemployment insurance, old-age pensions, and other reforms, many of which would be taken up by the new Roosevelt administration, elected a few weeks before. Dorothy was distressed that many journalists described the marchers as a collection of dangerous radicals. Even more, she was distressed that such a noble effort was organized by atheists and that the Catholic Church seemed distant from it. When the march had disbanded, Dorothy went to pray, on December 8, the feast day of the Immaculate Conception, at the National Shrine of the Immaculate Conception at Catholic University. "There I offered up a special prayer," she writes, "a prayer which came with tears and with anguish, that some way would open up for me to use what talents I possessed for my fellow workers, for the poor."[39]

6.2.2 The Catholic Worker

When Dorothy returned to her apartment (shared with her younger brother, John, and his wife, Tessa) she met Peter Maurin. As Dorothy recounts, Maurin said, "George Shuster, editor of *The Commonweal*, told me to look you up. Also, a red-haired Irish communist in Union Square told me to see you. He says we think alike."[40] Twenty years older than Dorothy, Maurin

37. Ibid., 61–62.
38. Forrest, *Love Is the Measure*, 52–53.
39. Day, *Long Loneliness*, 166.
40. Ibid., 169.

espoused what he called the "green revolution," and he was convinced that Dorothy was the collaborator he had been praying for. The son of a French peasant family, Peter had for nine years been a member of the Christian Brothers, a teaching order. He emigrated to Canada, where he homesteaded, worked in quarries, dug ditches, and labored in factories, mines, and lumber mills. He had the body and appearance of a middle-aged laborer and the mind of a visionary. He set about repairing Dorothy's education by teaching her about the saints. Real social change, he thought, would be grounded in sanctity and community. The immediate need, he said, was for a newspaper to publicize Catholic social teaching. Dorothy should be the editor.[41]

The first issue of the *Catholic Worker* was distributed on May 1, 1933. The Paulist Press printed 2,500 copies for $57. Dorothy set the price of the eight-page tabloid at a penny a copy—"to make it so cheap that anyone could afford to buy." Very soon contributions and orders began to come in; before the end of 1933, Maurin and Day were printing 75,000 copies. Clearly, other people shared Dorothy's desire to unite Catholicism with social reform.

Besides Bible quotations, Dorothy's editorials, and Peter Maurin's "Easy Essays" (pithy and poetic statements of his ideas), the paper reported on strikes, protests, union-building, child labor, and other topics often treated by radical newspapers. Peter Maurin resisted some of this. He thought the paper should devote itself to spreading the vision of a new society; they should promote an agrarian break with industrialism rather than supporting piecemeal attempts to ameliorate the worst excesses of capitalism. But over time it became clear that the *Catholic Worker* was more than just a leftist newspaper edited by Catholics; it promoted a vision of sanctity, community, and peace. Peter accommodated himself to Dorothy's direction of the paper.

Community led to hospitality. This was no accident, as Peter Maurin taught that hospitality ought to be practiced by all Christians. Donations allowed the purchase of an abandoned house where volunteers could prepare meals for street people, donated clothes could be sorted and given away, and the paper could be written. By 1936 there were thirty-three Catholic Worker houses spread across the country, and the New York house was feeding four hundred people a day. The Great Depression created an unending line of needy people.

In Catholic Worker houses, no one preached to the needy. There was no attempt to distinguish the "deserving" poor from the "undeserving." No attempts were made to reform or fix people. Crucifixes adorned the walls,

---

41. Forrest, *Love Is the Measure*, 56–59.

and if someone wanted to ask, the staff would try to explain why Christian doctrine required caring for the poor.

From the first issue of the *Catholic Worker*, Dorothy insisted on pacifism as part of Christian social teaching. For three years, this stand created no impediment to the growing movement. But in 1936 the civil war in Spain put the peace testimony to the test. On one side, socialists and communists supported the Republican forces in Spain; they saw the fight against Franco as one more step in a worldwide battle against authoritarian capitalism. On the other side, most Catholics in the United States supported Franco's Nationalists, since the church in Spain had allied itself with the general. The *Catholic Worker* refused to endorse the violence of either side. In particular, Dorothy took the U.S. church to task for its support of Franco, telling her readers to "look at recent events in Germany" to see where fascism would lead. She printed an essay by Jacques Maritain that warned of the anti-Semitism of fascism.[42] As a result, the *Catholic Worker* was disdained by those on the left and lost the financial support of many in the church. Bishops banned the paper in many dioceses. Circulation fell from 160,000 to 50,000 in less than a year.

Pacifism does not require neutrality. In the 1930s the *Catholic Worker* opposed the racism of the Nazis and published calls to let Jews freely immigrate to the United States—appeals that fell mostly on deaf ears. The failure of democratic nations to provide hospitality contributed to the holocaust.

When the United States entered World War II, the Catholic Worker maintained its pacifist stand. Dorothy wrote:

> We are still pacifists. Our manifesto is the Sermon on the Mount, which means that we will try to be peacemakers. Speaking for many of our conscientious objectors, we will not participate in armed warfare or in making munitions, or by buying government bonds to prosecute the war, or in urging others to these efforts.
>
> We love our country. . . . We have been the only country in the world where men and women of all nations have taken refuge from oppression.
>
> I would urge our friends and associates to care for the sick and the wounded, to the growing of food for the hungry, to the continuance of all our works of mercy in our houses and on our farms.[43]

42. Ibid., 72–73.

43. Ibid., 74–75.

Dorothy wrote "we," but in fact many members of the Catholic Worker movement could not agree. Donations dropped, houses closed, and young men volunteered for military service. Even the lines for meals at Catholic Worker houses shortened, because military conscription and a booming armaments industry absorbed millions of the unemployed. Dorothy Day never wavered. The paper continued promoting peace, sanctity, and community, and works of hospitality went on in those Catholic Worker houses that remained open.

After World War II came the Cold War and the Vietnam War. Dorothy, growing older, became an icon of the anti-war movement. For several years in the 1950s, New York City held civil defense drills that required everybody to report to air-raid shelters or face a $500 fine. Every year on the appointed day, Dorothy and others (the number of objectors grew yearly) protested by sitting in City Hall Park. "In the name of Jesus, who is God, who is Love, we will not obey this order to pretend, to evacuate, to hide," she wrote. "We will not be drilled into fear. . . . We do not have faith in God if we depend upon the Atom Bomb."[44] Each year they were arrested and those who would not pay the fine, such as Dorothy, were sentenced to jail. By 1960 the number of protesters had grown to 1,000, and even conservative newspapers editorialized that civil defense offered New Yorkers no protection against H-bombs. The police only arrested a symbolic handful of the protesters, avoiding Dorothy. In 1961 there were 2,000 protesters, and all over the city people defied the law. City officials gave up and ended the civil defense charade.

The *Catholic Worker* steadfastly opposed the Vietnam War. Many Catholic bishops supported the war, but Catholic thinking about war had shifted perceptibly since World War II. Many young Catholic men registered as conscientious objectors. The Catholic Peace Fellowship was formed. Daniel and Philip Berrigan were among many young Catholic leaders who protested the war. This is not to say that the church as a whole opposed the war; the great majority of the American church supported it. But pacifism no longer isolated the Catholic Worker movement inside the church.

The *Catholic Worker* applauded the nonviolence of Martin Luther King Jr. and rejoiced in the integration of buses in Montgomery, Alabama. In 1956 Dorothy visited Koinonia Farm, near Americus, Georgia, to show support for the interracial ministry led by protestant pastor Clarence Jordan. Koinonia had received threats, and some of its buildings had been machine-gunned. During her visit, Dorothy served as a sentry one night,

44. Ibid., 98.

sitting in a car. She saw a car approaching and ducked just before gunfire shattered the windows.[45]

The *Catholic Worker* supported Cesar Chavez and his efforts to unionize farm workers with a stream of articles and editorials from 1965 to 1978. The paper helped publicize United Farm Worker boycotts of table grapes, lettuce, raisins, and Gallo wines. In 1973, in California, Dorothy was arrested for the last time, for "remaining present at the place of a riot, rout and unlawful assembly"—that is, sitting on her foldable chair-cane while pleading with police not to hurt the picketers.[46]

During the Second Vatican Council, Dorothy joined in pilgrimage to Rome with the "fifty mothers for peace." Pope John XXIII, who called the Council, had published *Pacem in Terris* on April 11, 1963. Encouraged by the pope's call for an end to the arms race, the "mothers for peace" hoped for an audience with the pope and for the Council to take a stand for peace. John XXIII was ill, but the mothers did get to meet with Cardinal Augustin Bea. To their delight, the pope praised the "Pilgrims for Peace" at a public audience and blessed their work. John XXIII died a few weeks later. In 1965 the concluding document of the Second Vatican Council explicitly condemned "every act of war directed to the indiscriminate destruction of whole cities or vast areas."[47] It was the only specific condemnation pronounced by the Council.

In 1975 Dorothy retired from day-to-day management of the *Catholic Worker*, though she continued to contribute her column, "On Pilgrimage." She gave her last public talk in 1976. She died November 29, 1980.

6.3 REFLECTIONS ON THE CASES

Both Dorothy Day and William Wilberforce were Christians, they believed that their religious commitment required them to engage in social and political reform, and I have told their stories as exemplars of "faith." Therefore, to avoid confusion, I must point out that, speaking sociologically, there is no necessary connection between religious faith and the faith of the reformer. There have been plenty of social and political reformers who were atheists or agnostics. And there are plenty of faithful adherents of every religion who are mostly satisfied with the current social or political system and who oppose making changes to it. If someone like Wilberforce or Day claims that

45. Ibid., 102–3.
46. Ibid., 120–24.
47. Ibid., 108–12.

Christian faith requires the faithful to work for a better world (and both of them in fact did say this, again and again), she is making a *theological* claim. Sociologically, it is only accurate to say that religious faith pushes some believers to support reform; others will oppose it.

Wilberforce and Day illustrate my thesis that since faith tends to help persons achieve the internal goods of reform, faith is a virtue. Recall that in chapter 3 I said that the internal goods of social and political reform include at least two things: (1) a better understanding of central concepts relevant to social policy—concepts such as justice, wellbeing, human rights, autonomy, and virtue—and a better understanding of how these concepts can cohere, and (2) a better approximation of justice, wellbeing, and moral excellence in our actual social and political situation. Wilberforce and Day achieved these goods, and they did so despite opposition, frustrating setbacks, and misunderstanding by friends and foes. They both *believed* that the world could be changed for the better (in multiple ways), and they were *for* the changes they saw as necessary—they wanted change, they recommended change to others, they stood for change symbolically, and they hoped for change.

Given the opposition that Wilberforce and Day faced, it is equally clear that they had good reasons to doubt the things they believed. Wilberforce's faith included a *moral* belief—that slavery was wrong—and a belief about *social and political possibilities*—that slavery could be abolished. Wilberforce had to know rational, well-informed, and intelligent men who served in Parliament in the period 1787–1807 and who believed that the slave trade was not a moral evil and/or that the social and political reality made slavery impossible to eliminate. If Wilberforce had been an evidentialist, the reasons these men gave for their beliefs should have caused him to doubt his position. Wilberforce believed more strongly in his position than the evidentialist rule would permit. His *faith* greatly aided his pursuit of reform.

Similarly, Day met many people, including Catholics, who criticized the Catholic Worker movement on many points. The movement was accused of failing to discriminate between the deserving and undeserving poor, cooperating with atheists, undermining national security, giving comfort to radicals and criminals, subverting the rule of law, and so on. Day had to know that leading Catholics—intellectuals and bishops alike—often gave strong arguments against unionization in certain industries, or against welfare, or in favor of the U.S. war effort in Vietnam. Further, it is not clear that Day believed that the reform movements she supported could *succeed* anytime soon. She certainly did not expect to end poverty in America in her lifetime. Nevertheless, she believed that it was right to work to help the poor in a great variety of ways. She believed efforts to help the poor ought to pursue sanctity and community, so that poor people could be treated with dignity and not as mere recipients of charity. She believed it was right to do these things even though she knew churchpeople who disagreed. Her *faith* sustained her in seeking change.

Since Wilberforce pursued a legislative goal, his story seems to reach a victorious conclusion that Day's does not. Parliament criminalized the slave trade in 1807, and in subsequent decades effective enforcement actually ended it. In 1833 slavery was abolished in the British Empire, and a sum of twenty million pounds was appropriated to recompense West Indian owners for the loss of their slaves. Political action sometimes results in specific advances. The Catholic Worker movement did not focus on a supreme legislative goal (although at times the *Catholic Worker* would endorse a piece of legislation), so it is impossible to point to a signal achievement that indicates "success."

I think we should guard against the hasty conclusion that Wilberforce was more successful than Day. We should certainly reject the thesis that legislative means are always the best means by which to achieve reform. In some cases legislation will be an effective and viable route to change, but in other cases it won't. And legal changes must often be combined with deeper social change in order to be effective. The campaign against the slave trade illustrates this point; much of the work of the abolitionists focused on convincing the British people that the slave trade was morally wrong.

I suggest that success in social and political reform be judged not by political victories but by the two internal goods already identified. Did the reform effort lead to a better understanding of central concepts relevant to social policy? Did the reform effort lead to a better approximation of justice, wellbeing, and moral excellence in our actual social and political situation? I think the answer is yes for both Wilberforce and Day.

Justice has been recognized as a central concept in political philosophy since Plato and Aristotle. What is justice? How do we achieve it? The campaign against slavery helped us understand not only that slavery is unjust, but also that slavery can be eliminated. We no longer believe, as did ancient and medieval thinkers, that slavery must be accepted as part of the natural order of things. We know, of course, that slavery has not been eradicated. In the early twenty-first century, human trafficking continues to plague our world.[48] But many people today, like Wilberforce, understand that justice requires that we work to eliminate human trafficking.

Dorothy Day believed that a good society must care for poor people. The Catholic Worker movement translated that belief into many different,

---

48. For information on human trafficking in many countries, including the United States, see http://www.gvnet.com/humantrafficking.

specific actions. They supported government welfare programs, unionization of workers, hospitality houses for both men and women, education programs, communal farms, and so on. Some of these ideas didn't succeed; for instance, Catholic Worker farms usually had a shorter life span than was anticipated. Some of us might criticize Day for relying too heavily on a Marxist analysis of poverty that blames poverty on capitalism, not recognizing that it is the growth of capital that gives a society the power to reduce or eliminate poverty. I suggest we compare Day to Alfred Wegener. Just as Wegener's theory of continental displacement could be right on the central question of fixism versus mobilism and yet wrong on some details, so one could acknowledge Day's central belief—that a good society must care for the poor—while disagreeing with her on this or that detail. Reformers are often accused of being utopians and perfectionists, but the changes they bring about ought to be judged in terms of improvement, not perfection.

6.4 ON THE CONTENT OF BELIEFS

At various points in this book, I have mentioned the "objects" of our beliefs. I have relied on a vague description of the things we have faith in, saying that in the typical case faith involves believing "something" that other people, for whom one has intellectual respect, do not believe. At this point, having four real cases before us, we ought to notice how they fit that general description in different ways.

Alfred Wegener had faith in a *theory*. He believed that the continents moved and that this hypothesis helped explain data gathered from several earth sciences. The "object" of his belief could be described as a state of affairs in the physical world.

Henrietta Leavitt had faith$_{(7)}$ in that she relied on, or indwelt, subsidiary knowledge in the process of seeking focal knowledge. I think Leavitt also illustrates faith$_{(8)}$ in that she had faith in *herself*. She believed that her work—meticulously recording and analyzing the images on astrographic plates—was real science. She believed that patient attention to detail could produce scientific discovery and that the P-L relation she found was important. The object of her belief was the value of ability—her own ability to do science.

William Wilberforce had faith in a *cause*. He believed that slavery was wrong and that a campaign against slavery could bring about a distinct change: slavery could be eliminated. There were at least two parts to the object of his belief—a moral judgment and a belief about what was possible in society.

Dorothy Day also had faith in a *cause*, but that cause was more diffuse than Wilberforce's campaign against slavery. Day believed that a good society has to care for the poor. She probably did not believe poverty could be eliminated—certainly not in her time—but she believed it was still right to fight against it. Here the object of belief is almost purely moral, since Day believed the effort had to go on whether or not it succeeded.

Now each case can be described as *believing* a proposition and *being for* it. So each case fits the definition of faith given in chapter 2. But we notice that the propositions believed point to very different kinds of things, and this raises a possible criticism of my main argument. How can faith be a virtue, if the objects of faith can be as various as a hypothesis in natural science, the worth of one's work, possibilities of social change, and moral judgments?

In reply I make two points. First, we should notice that the evidentialist rule allows that *none* of these cases exhibit the virtue of faith, because faith is always vicious. Leavitt, Wegener, Wilberforce, and Day all believed beyond the evidence, so according to the evidentialist their beliefs are morally blameworthy. Now, I said in chapter 3 that a careful evidentialist would retreat a little from Clifford's overzealous statement: "It is wrong always, everywhere, and for anyone, to believe anything upon insufficient evidence." Instead, the careful evidentialist would admit that we believe background beliefs without evidence, but still condemn faith in other situations. But in regard to these cases the retreat does not help the careful evidentialist (for instance, Blackburn), because none of these cases involve background beliefs. So the evidentialist must condemn them all; they are all guilty of immoral believing.

Now I must make a philosophical move that I think is obvious and right. But it is so basic I can offer little to defend it, other than ask the reader to attend to the four cases I have presented. Here it is: Leavitt, Wegener, Wilberforce, and Day are *not* guilty of immoral believing. The careful evidentialist judgment against them is simply mistaken. Therefore, the "wide net" I have thrown over examples of faith only shows how wide-ranging and wrongheaded is evidentialism.

Second, I think the objects of faith really do vary from case to case. And this should make us wary. The main conclusion of the argument of this book is that faith is a virtue, that it contributes to good living. That does not mean that every possible example of faith$_{(8)}$ will be virtuous. We might say that Hitler had faith in himself, in a way at least superficially similar to Leavitt's faith. But Hitler's belief in himself was hardly part of a good life.

In the MacIntyrean schema we are using, a virtue helps people achieve the internal goods of practices. But practices must be judged by whether they can be incorporated into a life organized around a proper human *telos*. The reader will remember from chapter 1 how MacIntyre uses this fact to extend his definition of a virtue. Since human beings do not completely agree about the human *telos*, the good life consists partly in an ongoing debate over what the good life is, and virtues help sustain us in that debate. We don't need to have complete agreement in our long conversation about the good life to see that Leavitt's faith was virtuous while Hitler's was not.

Faith is a virtue. But not every example of "faith" (believing something and being for it) is a virtue. Once again we are reminded that in moral philosophy we have to pay attention to cases. As we do, we may gain wisdom as well as a better understanding of faith.

6.5 ON FAITH AND RISK

I have just said that faith$_{(8)}$ is a virtue, but not all examples that illustrate faith$_{(8)}$ are examples of virtue. This may seem confusing, so we should explore the matter more thoroughly.

Imagine a boy born in Germany in 1920. Imagine that as a teenager in the 1930s, this young man volunteers for the German army and joins the Nazi party. He is an intelligent and talented man; in the course of technical training (in engineering or architecture, for example) he comes into contact with persons and reading material that are critical of Hitler and Nazi doctrine. So our imagined young German is aware of other people, including experts in his own field, who do not agree with Nazi ideology. Nevertheless, he believes that Hitler is right and that Nazism is the salvation of Germany. He is *for* Nazism in many ways. According to the definition of faith$_{(8)}$ given in chapter 2, shouldn't we say that our imagined Nazi soldier has faith? But surely his faith is not a virtue. We can imagine that his faith in Hitler leads him to join the S.S. and participate actively in a death camp. To be a virtue, a trait must contribute to a good life, but the Nazi soldier's faith does not contribute to a good life. Therefore, faith is not a virtue.

This criticism does not refute my argument, but it does point to an important clarification. When I said, in chapter 2, that faith consists in believing and being for things that other people do not believe, I gestured toward what philosophers call a "necessary" condition, not a "sufficient" condition. That is, to be an example of faith$_{(8)}$ a trait must fit the description "believing and being for something that other people do not believe." But that is not enough to guarantee that the trait in question is a virtue. There may be traits—such as the belief and affections/volitions of the Nazi soldier—that match the definition of faith$_{(8)}$ and are not virtues. To be an example of real virtue, the faith of the Nazi soldier would have to be united with other elements; in particular, it must be compatible with the other virtues of a good life.

The previous paragraph makes a technical philosophical point. But the distinction has great practical importance. The moral life involves us, inevitably, in *risk*.

If we are to live good lives, we must believe things and be for them even when we know other people disagree with us. But *believing* and *being for* does not guarantee that we are right. We must face the awful truth: it is possible to give many years of one's life in support of some cause and then discover in one's later years that one no longer believes in that cause. It is possible to "wake up" and look back on one's life with intense moral regret.

The evidentialists will say that if we can't be sure that we are right, then we should not commit ourselves to action. That way, we will never have to look back with regret. They might claim that if we keep to our epistemic duty—"believe only in accord with the evidence"—we will also fulfill our moral duties.

But this advice will not work. Confronted with the evils of the slave trade and the weighty arguments that abolishing the slave trade would bankrupt Britain, many members of Parliament in Wilberforce's time adopted temporizing policies. Thus, by not acting to end the slave trade, they contributed to great evil. A refusal to commit oneself can lead one to look back on one's life with intense moral regret.

There is no safe path in the moral life. To live a good life, we must believe and we must be for the things we believe. *And our beliefs must be right.* Since there is no way to guarantee that our beliefs are right, we live with moral risk. I have argued that faith (that is, faith$_{(8)}$) is *necessary* for the good life; it is not, by itself, *sufficient* for the good life.

7

Faith as a Virtue in Parenting

In chapters 5 and 6 I briefly recounted the life stories of Henrietta Leavitt, Alfred Wegener, William Wilberforce, and Dorothy Day before describing their scientific or reform activities. I used these lives as illustrations of the way in which faith contributes to the success of MacIntyrean "practices." With each example, I first described the person's life before discussing his or her work. The division between life and work implied by that kind of arrangement was a bit forced even in those cases, because the practices of a person's life are interwoven. If we try to understand a person's life and character in parts—one practice or one virtue at a time—we may gain some insight, but we will probably also distort the whole picture. In any case, when it comes to parenting I will follow a different strategy. I will tell the story of two families and then make some comments on the role of faith in the practice of parenting.

7.1 THE MCBRIDE JORDAN FAMILY

The material in this section is drawn almost exclusively from James McBride's *The Color of Water: A Black Man's Tribute to His White Mother*, first published in 1996. *The Color of Water* occupied slots on the best-seller lists for two years, and it has been used as required reading in college classrooms. I expect, then, that some of my readers will be familiar with McBride's book. Perhaps for the others this little introduction will prompt them to read it.

The story begins with Rachel Dwajra Zylska, born April 1, 1921, in Poland to an Orthodox Jewish family. When she was two years old, her father, Fishel Zylska, moved the family (including an older brother, Samuel) to America. Fishel changed the family name to Shilsky, and Rachel became Rachel Deborah Shilsky. In America, Fishel Shilsky was an itinerant rabbi—apparently, not a very good one, as he was never invited to serve one congregation for very long. The family lived in several towns in New York and New Jersey before Fishel Shilsky decided to open a general store in Suffolk, Virginia, when Rachel was eight or nine years old.

Growing up in a small Virginia town during the hard days of the Great Depression, Rachel witnessed discrimination against blacks—and religious discrimination against Jews that was only slightly less virulent. Among the white population, the Jews suffered isolation and rejection; Rachel had only one friend in her school years, a white girl named Frances. At school, Rachel began calling herself Ruth. She thought it sounded less Jewish.

Fishel Shilsky was a hard, calculating man. He profited by serving as rabbi to the Jewish population of the area (by supervising kosher animal slaughtering, for instance), by selling goods to African Americans in his store (despising blacks, he regularly overcharged them), and by catering to the white population on Sunday (because he observed the Sabbath, his store was the only one in town open on Sunday). He did not love his wife, Hudis, whom he had married in an arranged marriage in Poland. Hudis had polio when she was young, which left her partially crippled on her left side. Fishel ridiculed Hudis's appearance and physical inabilities in the presence of her children.

Fishel Shilsky sexually abused Rachel/Ruth, so that she lived in terror of her father's presence at night as much as his harsh discipline during the day. Hudis, in spite of her physical limitations, strove mightily to maintain a kosher Jewish household. She loved her children (a younger daughter, Gladys, was born in America), but Hudis was dependent on her husband and able to give her children only limited protection. Since Hudis did not speak English, Ruth translated for her.

At fifteen, Ruth fell in love with Peter, a young black man who often visited the store. Naturally, she hid this relationship from her racist father. Ruth became pregnant—quite likely a death sentence for Peter if the truth became public. Both teenagers were terrified of the Klan. Hudis overheard the lovers' despairing talk and sent Ruth to New York, to her younger sister, Betsy; Aunt Betts helped Ruth obtain an abortion. A year later, when Ruth returned to Suffolk, she found that Peter had impregnated another girlfriend, this time a young black woman whom he could marry.

Graduating high school in 1939, Ruth left Suffolk for New York City the next day. For a long time she regretted deserting her mother, but she had to get away from her father and the suffocating racism of Virginia. Her brother Sam had already escaped the family and joined the army. He died in World War II.

In New York, Ruth worked in a leather factory owned by another aunt, Mary. There she met Andrew Dennis McBride, a young African American newly arrived from North Carolina. A violinist, he had tried to support himself as a musician, but orchestras would not hire blacks. Eventually he turned to factory work. In Ruth's words,

> Well, Dennis was a solid, clean Christian man. He seemed to understand me and see right through me. It wasn't long before I fell in love with him and after a few months we started thinking of getting married. Well, *I* started thinking of getting married. Dennis hemmed and hawed on it . . .[1]

Back home in North Carolina, McBride knew, he could be murdered for marrying a white woman. New York City was different, but how different? In 1940 he consented to live with Ruth, though the couple did not marry until 1942. Ruth visited Dennis's North Carolina relatives, but not accompanied by her husband—at least, not until 1957. That was when Dennis died, and she took his body home for burial.

Through Aunt Mary, Ruth's family learned that she was living with a black. They went through rituals of mourning, and thereafter considered her dead. Hudis Shilsky died in 1942, cutting Ruth's last tie to her Jewish roots. Ruth professed faith in Jesus and joined the Metropolitan Baptist Church, a large African American church in Harlem. For the rest of her life, her friends and social connections were mostly drawn from her black husbands' extended families and African American Christian churches.

The McBrides' first child, Andrew Dennis McBride, was born in 1943. They would have seven more; Ruth was pregnant with the last, James, when her husband died. At first they lived in a one-room apartment in Harlem, later moving to the Red Hook Housing Project in Brooklyn.

Dennis McBride felt a calling to Christian ministry. He earned a Divinity degree in 1953, and in 1954 the couple started New Brown Memorial Baptist Church not far from Red Hook. (The church was named for Rev. Abner Brown of Metropolitan Baptist, who had married them.) Both the family and the church were desperately poor. "God just provided somehow," Ruth later told James.[2]

In 1957 Dennis McBride died of lung cancer. His death left Ruth with seven children and one yet to be born, no insurance, and no income. But

---

1. McBride, *Color of Water*, 195–96.
2. Ibid., 240.

Ruth's social connections to the "black side" were still in place. After burying her husband in North Carolina, Ruth returned to find her post office box stuffed with gifts from friends, relatives, and people from the church. Dennis's aunt Candis moved from rural North Carolina to New York, which she had never so much as visited, to help Ruth manage her children. The funeral gifts were quickly spent, and Ruth forced herself to approach her white relatives for help—appeals that were rebuffed. Ruth explains,

> When Jews say kaddish, they're not responsible for you anymore. You're dead to them. Saying kaddish and sitting shiva, that absolves them of any responsibility for you. I was on my own then, but I wasn't alone, because like Dennis said, God the Father watched over me, and sent me your stepfather, who took over and he saved us and did many, many things for us. He wasn't a minister like Dennis. He was different, a workingman who had never been late for work in the thirty years that he worked for the New York City Housing Authority, and he was a good, good man.[3]

Ruth's marriage to Hunter L. Jordan produced four more children. Hunter Jordan spent his life savings to buy a house for Ruth and her children in the St. Albans neighborhood of Queens. During the workweek, Jordan continued to live in his small house on Carlton Avenue in Brooklyn, joining the family in Queens on the weekends. He was an older man who couldn't endure the noise and confusion of the family on a continual basis. As a weekend parent he repaired things, brought home groceries, and provided a measure of calm in a seemingly chaotic household. McBride writes:

> He made no separation between the McBride and Jordan children, and my siblings and I never thought of or referred to each other as half brothers and sisters; for the powerless Little Kids, myself included, he was "Daddy." For the midlevel executives, he was sometimes "Daddy," sometimes "Mr. Hunter." To the powerful elder statesmen who remembered their biological father well, he was always "Mr. Hunter."[4]

Hunter Jordan died of a stroke at age seventy-two, when James McBride was fourteen. Ruth worked evenings at Chase Manhattan Bank, arriving home at 2 A.M. She appointed the oldest resident child as "queen" or "king" of the household in her absence, but in reality Ruth was very much in charge of the family. The system continued to work even after

3. Ibid., 246.
4. Ibid., 118–19.

Hunter Jordan's death. Ruth and Dennis had determined the family rules long before:

> He [Dennis McBride] left behind no insurance policy, no dow-
> ry, no land, no money for his pregnant wife and young children,
> but he helped establish the groundwork for Ma's raising twelve
> children which lasted thirty years—kids not allowed out after
> five o'clock; stay in school, don't ever follow the crowd, and fol-
> low Jesus—and as luck, or Jesus, would have it, my stepfather
> helped Mommy enforce those same rules when he married her.[5]

Church and school: these were the twin priorities of the McBride
Jordan house. James McBride recounts his memories of Ruth regularly
bringing five or six children to New Brown Memorial Baptist Church (older
siblings being away at college), where they attended Sunday school and were
strongly encouraged to participate in worship by reciting Scripture, singing,
or playing instruments.

Ruth was determined that her children succeed in school and go to
college. She drilled into them the importance of training their minds. She
scheduled time for homework and often reviewed a child's work after getting home from the bank at 2 A.M. And there was something else . . .

> Every year the mighty bureaucratic dinosaur known as the
> New York City Public School System would belch forth a tiny
> diamond: they slipped a little notice to parents giving them the
> opportunity to have their kids bused to different school districts
> if they wanted; but there was a limited time to enroll, a short
> window of opportunity that lasted only a few days. Mommy
> stood poised over that option like a hawk. She invariably chose
> predominantly Jewish public schools: P.S. 138 in Rosedale, J.H.S
> 231 in Springfield Gardens, Benjamin Cardozo, Francis Lewis,
> Forest Hills, Music and Art [High School]. Every morning we
> hit the door at six-thirty, fanning out across the city like soldiers,
> armed with books, T squares, musical instruments, an "S" bus
> pass that allowed you to ride the bus and subway for a nickel,
> and a free-school-lunch coupon in our pocket.[6]

Ruth's ties to her Jewish family were cut, but she had absorbed Judaism's
respect for education. Even her abusive father had paid for tutors to make
sure his daughters learned what he thought important, since he didn't trust
Virginia schools. Ruth, on the other hand, did trust those public schools

5. Ibid., 251.
6. Ibid., 88.

that served New York's Jewish enclaves. Often, of course, her policy of send-
ing her children to distant schools meant that they became lone black faces
in white classrooms. On the surface, at least, Ruth McBride Jordan simply
ignored the questions of racial identity that were thrust onto her children.
White and black did not matter to Ruth; the important things were God and
education.

> One afternoon [when James McBride was in first grade] as we
> walked home from the bus stop, I asked Mommy why she didn't
> look like the other mothers.
>
> "Because I'm not them," she said.
>
> "Who are you?" I asked.
>
> "I'm your mother."
>
> "Then why don't you look like Rodney's mother, or Pete's
> mother? How come you don't look like me?"
>
> She sighed and shrugged. She'd obviously been down this
> road many times. "I do look like you. I'm your mother. You ask
> too many questions. Educate your mind. School is important.
> Forget Rodney and Pete. Forget their mothers. You remember
> school. Forget everything else. Who cares about Rodney and
> Pete! When they go one way, you go the other way. Understand?
> When they go one way, you go the other way. You hear me?"
>
> "Yes."
>
> "I know what I'm talking about. Don't follow none of them
> around. You stick to your brothers and sisters, that's it. Don't tell
> nobody your business neither!" End of discussion.[7]

"Don't tell nobody your business neither!" It seems that Ruth thought
privacy could shield her children from some of the hurts that a race-conscious society would inflict on them. Whether it was white racism in the
dominant culture or the Black Power movement of the 1960s, Ruth had no
time for it:

> Her motto was, "If it doesn't involve your going to school or
> church, I could care less about it and my answer is no whatever
> it is." She insisted on absolute privacy, excellent school grades,
> and trusted no outsiders of either race.[8]

7. Ibid., 12–13.
8. Ibid., 27.

The family was always poor. Ruth and her husbands prized spiritual values and educated minds above material things, while at the same time displaying great determination and creativity in meeting their children's needs. The boys slept three to a bed in one room; the girls shared in another. Clothes, books, and musical instruments were passed down from sibling to sibling. The children ate free lunches at school. Ruth kept tabs on community events at zoos, parks, schools, libraries, and churches, often leading her young troupe across the city to take advantage of a free block party, lecture, concert, or exhibit. Twice a year she took them to a free dental clinic, where interns practiced their developing skills. Chase Manhattan Bank, where Ruth worked, served complimentary dinner to employees; Ruth stuffed her purse with sandwich makings to supplement the household food supply. Early in their school years, all the children learned how to navigate their way around the city on "S" bus passes. And so on. As Ruth said, "God just provided somehow."

Ruth's privacy rule extended to—or maybe was founded in—her own past. She routinely pushed aside her children's questions about her race or her family. "I'm light-skinned," she would respond. Or "I do look like you. I'm your mother. You ask too many questions. Educate your mind." At the same time, they saw her react angrily or even violently to examples of racism: the white shopowner who sold her son spoiled milk, the school officials who asked at parent-teacher conferences if her children were adopted, and many other examples. James McBride writes that as a boy he feared for his mother, a little white woman living in the projects. Unlike most whites, Ruth seemed at ease among African Americans in the projects. She kept her Jewish background almost entirely secret from her children until they were grown.

The family could not escape the stresses of the culture around it. The Black Power movement of the sixties, the drug culture of the streets, teen culture, and the ordinary stresses of growing up all compounded the identity questions the McBride Jordan children faced. Some of them staged "revolutions"; they rebelled against Ruth's rules for a few months or years. After Hunter Jordan died, James McBride started cutting school, smoking and selling marijuana, and committing minor burglaries. A sister, Helen, ran away when she was fifteen. A brother, Richie, got married at eighteen despite Ruth's objections, then divorced, and then entered college. McBride's oldest brother, Dennis, while making his way through college and medical school (thus pleasing Ruth immensely), risked his life by participating in civil rights marches and sit-ins (while keeping this side of his life secret from his mother).

And yet, in spite of the obstacles—poverty, the lure of the streets, the racism of individuals and institutions—the McBride Jordan children fulfilled the vision their parents had for them:

> My parents were nonmaterialistic. They believed that money without knowledge was worthless, that education tempered with religion was the way to climb out of poverty in America, and over the years they were proven right.[9]

James and his brothers and sisters survived their adolescent rebellions. All twelve McBride Jordan children graduated from college; they earned at least twelve postgraduate degrees between them. The McBride Jordan family produced two doctors, a computer consultant, a journalist, a history professor, a chemistry professor, a social worker, a nurse, two teachers, a medical office manager, and a customer service manager.

Ruth herself went to college and graduated from Temple University in 1986, to add another social worker to the list. After retirement, she lived with one of her daughters, Kathy, in Ewing, New Jersey. She volunteered at a homeless shelter, a reading club, and the food program of Jerusalem Baptist Church. She died January 9, 2010.

THE BOULDING FAMILY

My interest in this section is in Kenneth and Elise Boulding's family, but I will start with a brief review of their work as academics and scholars. I hope to encapsulate their public lives so that I can then focus on their family life.

Born in 1910, Kenneth Boulding was an economist who refused to accept narrow boundaries for his discipline. He thought economics should be conceived as part of generalized social science; he brought insights into economics from mathematics, biology, systems theory, philosophy, and peace research. He first published in 1932, while still a student, in an economics journal edited by J. M. Keynes. In 1941 he published *Economic Analysis*, which became a standard textbook of conventional economic theory. By 1950, however, he was broadening his approach to economics, developing what became known in the 1970s as "evolutionary economics." Boulding emphasized the role of knowledge, its growth and transmission, in a social/economic system—"know-how" replaces the economists' narrower term *capital*. Since the social/economic system is part of a planetary ecology, Boulding thought economics needed to pay attention to environmental limitations; he welcomed Buckminster Fuller's concept of "spaceship earth."

9. Ibid., 29.

Boulding was an academic organizer. While on faculty at the University of Michigan, he established the Center for Research in Conflict Resolution. Later, at the University of Colorado, he founded the Center for Advanced Study in the Behavioral Sciences. At different times he served as president of the American Economic Association, the Society for General Systems Research, and the American Association for the Advancement of Science. He won scholarly prizes in economics, political science, peace research, and research in the humanities.

Boulding wrote poetry (e.g., *There Is a Spirit: The Nayler Sonnets*, 1945), social philosophy (e.g., *Beyond Economics: Essays on Society, Religion, and Ethics*, 1968), and peace studies (e.g., *Conflict and Defense: A General Theory*, 1962). He thoroughly rejected the notion that economics could be a nonnormative science; he insisted that moral commitments must enliven all social science.

Though perhaps not as prolific an academic writer as her husband, Elise Boulding wrote books in sociology (e.g., *Building a Global Civic Culture: Education for an Interdependent World*, 1988), peace studies (e.g., *Cultures of Peace: The Hidden Side of History*, 2000), and women's studies (e.g., *The Underside of History: A View of Women through Time*, 1976). She contributed hundreds of articles to scholarly and religious journals.

Perhaps that is enough to introduce the Bouldings as important social scientists. Now I will try to describe the Bouldings' family, rather than their academic accomplishments. To that end, I will draw most of the material for this section from Mary Morrison's 2005 biography of Elise Boulding, *A Life in the Cause of Peace*, and Elise Boulding's collection of essays on family life, *One Small Plot of Heaven*.

In 1923 an economic downturn in Norway prompted a young engineer, Josef Bjorn-Hansen, to immigrate to the United States. He brought with him his wife, Birgit, and their three-year-old daughter, Elise. Birgit's younger sister, Tulla, quickly followed them to America, but she died soon after. Birgit was heartbroken and unhappy in America; she longed to return to Norway. The family stayed in America, however, returning to Norway only for a visit, when Elise was ten.

Two more daughters were born to the Bjorn-Hansens—the first when Elise was nine years old, and the second when she was eleven. Thus, Elise spent much of her childhood as an only child and close companion of her mother, who greatly influenced her daughter. Birgit treasured Norwegian culture; after school, she insisted that Elise do her homework in Norwegian as well as in English so that Elise would know the language. As a young woman in Norway, Birgit had been something of a radical, organizing women's clubs and joining peace marches. Elise imbibed many of her mother's beliefs—that Norway was a safe place, that women should be educated and have opportunities outside the home, and that war was wrong.

Birgit thought American culture was crassly materialistic, unappreciative of art and music. As an immigrant, she never felt at home in her new country. At the same time, she pushed her daughters to achieve great things in their new land; she insisted that they play musical instruments (Elise played cello) and do well in school. Mary Morrison quotes Elise as saying,

> I must have the best, the most constructive and culturally developed environment and contacts at all times, because I was going to grow up and to achieve great things in America. We belonged to the last great wave of immigrants, but we were not just any old immigrants, we were *Norwegians* . . .
>
> . . . I must always carry myself like a Norseman, walk erect, and look people in the eye. I was also trained to great politeness. I had to curtsey to adults in a country where no one curtsied anymore. Mother had a program of toughening me up which involved sloshing ice water over me each morning before I got out of bed.[10]

After high school, Elise attended the New Jersey College for Women, now named Douglas College and part of Rutgers University. She majored in English and for the first time began to think of becoming a serious scholar. She continued to play cello, sometimes in the homes of faculty, and these "musical evenings" led to extended discussions between students and faculty in informal settings. Such intellectual discussions in informal, family settings would later be replicated in the Boulding household.

As Norwegians, Elise's family was nominally Lutheran, but they rarely attended church. As a young girl Elise was taught the Lord's Prayer, which she recited every night in Norwegian, and Christmases were celebrated joyously. Beyond that, Elise was left to pursue religion on her own. From an early age she felt a profound sense of God's presence in times of solitude, particularly in the outdoors. While a schoolgirl, Elise began attending a Protestant church near the Boulding home. The minister's wife, Mrs. Northwood, befriended Elise and invited her to tea. Mrs. Northwood became a mentor, treating the girl and her questions with respect. Elise's early experiences of religious solitude and her gratitude for Mrs. Northwood's companionship were reflected later in Elise's writings about children's spirituality. In her college years, Elise visited Catholic churches and Quaker meetings.

In 1940 Germany invaded Norway, shattering Elise's image, inherited from her mother, of that country as a safe refuge. The realization that

10. Morrison, *Elise Boulding*, 30.

there was no safe place in the world intensified her concern for peacemaking. Upon graduating from college, Elise moved to New York City for five months, an unsettling period in her personal life, as she experienced for the first time tedious office work and what she considered superficial office parties and gossip. While in New York, she visited a Catholic Worker house and was greatly impressed by Catherine de Hueck, a Russian émigré who had given away great wealth to live a life of service among the very poor. The months in New York were a time of "reckoning" as Elise sorted through the values inherited from her family. Elise's exposure to the Quakers and the Catholic Worker movement reinforced the pacifist leanings she had picked up from her mother.

In 1941 Elise moved to Syracuse, New York, escaping the big city and rejoining her family, who had relocated there. She began attending the local Quaker meeting, where she met an Englishman, Kenneth Boulding. He was ten years her senior, already a well-known economic theorist, and author of *Economic Analysis*, published that same year. She recalled:

> I met Kenneth Boulding at a Quaker meeting for worship. The signals were so clear to both of us (and apparently to the entire Quaker community of upstate New York) that we were to share our lives, that we announced our intentions of marriage only seventeen days after we met.
>
> While in one way I had been preparing for the world Kenneth Boulding introduced me to all my life, in another way this was a new world to me. . . . Kenneth's own deep spirituality released the last of my own inhibitions about the religious dimension. He was himself going through a period of great religious stress at that time, suffering because his family back in England was enduring the bombing raids from Germany while he was sitting safe in America. His intellectual analysis of the futility of war and his religious commitment to peace combined to produce, during the course of the year we met, the first in a long series of books . . .[11]

In one of Kenneth's sonnets, written to honor another couple's wedding, he described a Quaker home as "one small plot of heaven." He and Elise consciously adopted that sentiment as the goal of their own marriage. They envisioned making a home that exhibited love, hospitality, and peace:

> Kenneth and I took the founding of our little Quaker "colony of heaven," as he later described marriage in his "Sonnet for a Quaker Wedding," both seriously and joyfully. We did indeed

11. Boulding, *One Small Plot of Heaven*, 53.

endeavor to make our home a center of tranquility and peace, that all who entered might find refreshment therein, according to the old Quaker advice. It was always a community center, and when the children came it was a children's center too.[12]

Over the years, Kenneth continued to compose love sonnets to Elise. Many of them were published, privately, as *Sonnets for Elise* (1957).

The Bouldings had five children: Russell (b. 1947); Mark (b. 1949); Christine (b. 1951); Philip (b. 1953); and William (b. 1955). It was a busy, sometimes pressured, life. The 1950s and 1960s were some of Kenneth's most productive years as an academic organizer and publishing scholar. Both parents were active leaders and frequent public speakers among Quakers, and Elise taught Sunday school almost the entire time. Elise wrote frequently for Quaker publications. She earned a master's degree in 1949, with a published study of the effects of wartime separation on Iowa families during World War II.

From the beginning of their marriage, Kenneth and Elise were concerned to promote peacemaking. They *preached* peace in Quaker meetings and various public gatherings; they were peace *activists*, encouraging the passage of legislation such as the Voting Rights Act and urging support for the United Nations, while opposing atom bomb testing and the war in Vietnam; and between them they practically invented peace *research* as an academic field. As noted above, Kenneth founded the Center for Research in Conflict Resolution at the University of Michigan; Elise served as president of the International Peace Research Association.

At home, the Bouldings encouraged their children to settle conflicts nonviolently, though as Elise remembered, "with turbulent boys it was not always easy."[13] They practiced a daily time of worship before meals—sometimes with music or Scripture readings, but most often with silence. Drawing on her own experience of spiritual silence as a child, Elise encouraged the children to have time alone. They allowed the children a great deal of freedom to explore their interests. Sometimes this provoked criticism:

> A fellow Quaker who knew her during that time related that when Elise spoke about parenting at Quaker gatherings, others felt the Boulding children were not as "disciplined" as they should be and that it was somewhat ironic that Elise should be speaking on how to parent when the perception was that her own children were somewhat out of control! Philosophically, Elise believed in giving her children a certain amount of

12. Ibid., 54.
13. Ibid.

freedom, and, with five young children, disciplining at times took a back seat to other activities.[14]

The Boulding children remembered their parents listening to them and taking them seriously to a degree they did not observe in their friends' homes. Having publicly prominent parents, the children felt unspoken expectations to "make a contribution."[15] But the children were not pressured into academic careers, nor did they feel they had to be peace activists. The youngest child, William, became an economics professor, but the others became what Russell called "entrepreneurs" of one sort or another: Russell an environmental consultant and subsistence farmer, Mark the owner of an artistic display company, Christine the vice president and CFO of a contracting company, and Philip a musician and instrument maker.[16]

In the beginning, Kenneth and Elise accepted traditional gender roles in their marriage. Kenneth was the provider and Elise the homemaker. The door to Kenneth's home office was often shut while he worked, leaving much of the active parenting to Elise. In a 1997 interview, Russell related the following:

> My father in many ways was not real present to us as children. I think he had a wonderful sense of playfulness, but I remember my mother once commenting to me that she used to get exasperated with my father when we were young and playing with blocks, essentially it would be like parallel play. . . . He would get so involved in building these wonderful towers out of blocks, they would go all the way to the ceiling, he wasn't really playing *with* us.[17]

In later years, some feminists criticized Elise for not opposing more strongly traditional gender roles, seeing them as patriarchal patterns of oppression. As Quakers, Elise and Kenneth certainly believed in equality between the sexes, and Elise contributed important research to women's studies, as noted above. At every stage of their lives together, Elise was active in community and Quaker activities outside the home. But Elise thought that too often feminists disparaged the homemaker's role because they accepted the notion that traditional "male" roles are more important than the nurturing roles traditionally assigned to women. Elise, deeply involved in parenting while at the same time active in many church and peacemaking

14. Morrison, *Elise Boulding*, 55.
15. Ibid., 57.
16. Ibid., 59.
17. Ibid., 61.

activities, believed that a deep connection exists between nurturance and peace.

There has been a long tradition of thought that peace between the nations can be attained through some form of intergovernmental organization. William Penn and Immanuel Kant are historical examples of such thinking, and organizations like the League of Nations and the United Nations have grown out of it. Kenneth and Elise Boulding certainly approved of intergovernmental efforts to negotiate international disputes and broker peaceful settlements. However, Elise Boulding emphasized developmental and cultural aspects of peacemaking. The family unit, she thought, with its power to shape the worldview of children, is crucial to building a culture of peace. In an essay titled "The Family as a Practice Ground in Making History," she wrote,

> During my years as a college professor with a number of national and international committee and task force assignments, I increasingly came to feel the relevance of my previous twenty-five years apprenticeship in homemaking and community activism. . . . When we talk of "making history," we often think of dramatic public acts. Yet, history is really made by the painstaking accumulation of different kinds of experiences and skills in private and public settings.[18]

Much of Elise Boulding's peace research focused on building a world culture of peace. She emphasized the role of nongovernmental organizations (NGOs), such as the Red Cross, the Boy Scouts and Girl Scouts, or international women's groups, in building shared understandings around the world. Just as families instruct children to seek peace, such organizations can help people all over the world grow into a culture of peace. Elise wrote as a sociologist; her belief in the importance of the family reflected not only her own experience but also years of research:

> Receiving love and acceptance in early childhood, experiencing times of solitary reflection in puberty and adolescence, accepting early responsibility for self and others—this combination seems to produce peacemakers. Always we come back to what is happening in that most intimate setting of our lives, the household.[19]

The Boulding household often included one or two college students who, in exchange for room and board, would contribute to housework or

18. Boulding, *One Small Plot of Heaven*, 159.
19. Ibid., 118.

child care. These live-in guests were part of a broader program of hospitality. The Bouldings sometimes hosted informal discussions, somewhat like the "musical evenings" of Elise's college years. Earlier, during their time in Ann Arbor, while Kenneth was on faculty at the University of Michigan, the Bouldings were very close to five other families in the Quaker meeting there. Elise wrote:

> To this day we are one huge extended family, traveling any distance to be together for special life events like the next generation's marriages. We were all equally active in the peace movement and in local community action projects. While we were also concerned with the nurture of the inward life in our families and meeting, the community action often got in the way. I was not the only young mother in the community who had a need to justify her existence! There was, I believe, undue busyness.[20]

For Elise, this "undue busyness" eventually produced a spiritual crisis, which came to a head in the early 1970s. Twenty-five years of parenting, activism, and scholarship had produced a state of mental and physical exhaustion. In her fifties she relearned to make space in her life for solitude, taking retreats at monasteries and spending a year (1974) living much of the time alone in a one-room hermitage cabin on a mountain above the family cabin in the Colorado forest. She visited Kenneth and others on weekends and even attended a few meetings, but mostly she attended to God. After the hermitage year, Elise often returned for weekends and other respites.

The Bouldings' marriage of more than fifty years ended with Kenneth's death in 1993. In 1996 Elise moved to Massachusetts to be closer to her daughter Christine. By this time she had laid down leadership roles in national and international peace and women's groups. In 2000 she moved into a rest-care facility, though she continued to be active in local Quaker and educational groups. She died on June 24, 2010.

7.3 REFLECTIONS ON THE CASES

The McBride Jordan case and the Boulding case illustrate and extend some of the comments I made about faith in the practice of parenting in chapter 3. The reader will recall these four points. First, I suggested that there is a *telos* to the practice of parenting, that is, that parents aim at producing human excellence in their children, even if most parents would never use such

20. Ibid., 55.

philosophical language to describe their aims. Second, there is an internal good of parenting: the joy and satisfaction experienced by parents as they see progress being made by their children.[21] Third, I said that faith enables success in parenting by allowing parents to steer their course toward certain goals even though they know other people disagree with the goals they have adopted. Fourth, and more importantly, faith enables parents to persist in their project of parenting in the face of various obstacles. Let's consider the McBride Jordan family and the Boulding family in regard to these four points.

Ruth McBride Jordan and her husbands might be said to have very concrete goals in their parenting. Every child was expected to go to college and to have a respectable career. James McBride obviously reflects family pride—and specifically, his mother's satisfaction—when at the end of his memoir he lists the degrees and career successes of all twelve McBride Jordan children. But that tells only part of the tale. Readers of *The Color of Water* recognize that academic and career successes are important markers of a less quantifiable success in the McBride Jordan story. These adult children love their mother. James McBride alludes to boisterous family weekends attended by many parts of the extended family, with Ruth the cherished matriarch. Her children's careers show them to be servants of the wider community. They are an interracial family that has triumphed to a significant degree in a race-conscious society.

Kenneth and Elise Boulding explicitly thought of their home as a "colony of heaven." They wanted to make a place of peace, hospitality, and spiritual refreshment. They desired to raise nonviolent children who would become peacemakers. They hoped that guests, including live-in college students, would find in their home pointers to God and peace. To use a phrase from Elise's later work, their home was to be a microcosm of a "global civic culture of peace."

Perhaps most parents are not as explicit in naming their parenting goals as were Ruth McBride Jordan and the Bouldings. But parents can pursue a *telos* without being able to put it into words. As a philosopher, I have

21. Remember that MacIntyre defines an internal good as a good made possible only by the practice in question, or by some very similar practice. External goods like money and prestige can be gained in many ways, but the satisfactions of chess are only available through chess or similar games. In this regard it is worth noting that people sometimes say of success in some activity that it is like seeing children succeed. For example, someone starts a business that continues after the founder has left, and the founder expresses her delight by saying that it feels as if her child is walking on his own. The fact that we use such expressions shows that we assume other people are familiar with the satisfaction of successful parenting—and that they prize that satisfaction very highly indeed.

given a very general, abstract label to this *telos*; parents seek to produce "human excellence." Notice that in practice this general description can look very different in concrete cases. For instance, Ruth McBride Jordan did not share the Bouldings' value of nonviolence; she used corporal punishment on her children and advised them to respond to violence with violence: "If somebody hits you, take your fist and *crack* 'em."[22]

We don't have direct testimony that these parents experienced the internal goods of parenting, which I have described as joy and satisfaction resulting from seeing children succeed. Indirectly, however, I think both stories indicate that the Bouldings and Ruth McBride Jordan felt such goods. They looked on their adult children with pride, love, and gratitude. Of course, these two families are hardly exceptional in this regard; many, many people have experienced the internal goods of parenting. How could it be otherwise? If a society does not have at least a measure of success in parenting, conceived as a MacIntyrean practice, it cannot endure.

Both families had to know that other people would condemn the goals they had set for raising their children. When Dennis and Ruth McBride married in 1942, interracial marriage was illegal in some states. Most Americans, white and black, thought interracial marriage was morally wrong, or at least seriously unwise, precisely because it would produce mixed-race children. Many people would have considered Dennis and Ruth's project of defeating racial barriers through religion and education naïve. That Ruth often seemed to deny her own whiteness would strike some as bizarre, perhaps even pathological.

The Bouldings wanted to raise nonviolent children who would become peacemakers—and this in 1950s and '60s America, during McCarthyism, the Cold War, "duck and cover" civil defense drills in grade schools, and the Vietnam War. Kenneth, Elise, and the other Quaker parents in their Ann Arbor meeting were quite conscious of raising their children to live counterculturally, to reject important values of the culture around them.

In both cases, then, the visions of human excellence by which the parents raised their children were controversial. They had to know that other people—well-informed, rational, morally serious people—disapproved of their projects. Nevertheless, these parents *believed* in the goals they had set for their families, and they clearly acted *for* those goals in many different ways. Therefore, both sets of parents exhibited *faith* in their goals.

Remember again the evidentialist rule. The evidentialists tell us it is immoral to believe something more strongly than the evidence suggests. The practice of parenting shows how erroneous this rule is. My point is not

22. McBride, *Color of Water*, 9.

merely that the McBride Jordan and Boulding families rightfully violated this rule. It would seem that all good parents do. Parenting in a world in which rational people seriously disagree about the proper goals of parenting (and thus supply evidence against one's understanding of proper parenting) seems to require that good parents violate the evidentialist rule. How could we possibly direct our children toward excellence if we do not believe in goals that some people do not regard as excellent?

The previous paragraph focuses what we might call a *philosophical* problem, that is, disagreement about the proper goals of parenting, conceived abstractly. Faith is a virtue in regard to that question. But a more important role for faith comes when we consider the *practical* obstacles of the real world.

Ruth McBride Jordan raised twelve biracial children in New York in the 1950s and 1960s. They were exposed to the sexual revolution (which Ruth, as a conservative Christian, opposed), street crime, gangs, and drug use, from marijuana to alcohol to heroin. Hanging over everything was America's greatest social sin, pervasive racism, which disapproved of the very existence of those children. Each one of the McBride Jordan children had to confront his or her own questions of racial identity while negotiating the ordinary turbulence of adolescence in the midst of a country fighting with itself over the issue of race.

Despair is a fatal vice in parenting. If Ruth had given up on a child in the face of some setback—James McBride makes clear there were many setbacks, only some of which Ruth became aware of—that child might well have been lost. Against all the obstacles, Ruth continued to believe her children could succeed. Clearly, her faith helped achieve success in parenting.

Remember that on MacIntyre's account, a virtue is a trait that *tends* to enable success in a practice. James McBride's book is charming partly because all twelve McBride Jordan children finished college and went on to successful careers. Such overwhelming success is not required for the argument of this book. Suppose one or more of Ruth's children had died in a gunfight over drug money. We should still count her faith as a MacIntyrean virtue if it improved the likelihood of success.

The Bouldings did not face the same obstacles. They raised their children in comfortable suburban settings replete with the cultural and educational opportunities of major universities. The Boulding children learned about racism and poverty as social problems to be combated, not as personal threats. Nevertheless, the Bouldings needed faith to persevere in the project of parenting. In a sense, the obstacles faced by the Bouldings were created by their high vision of what their family should be. In that vision, their home was to be much more than a safe nest serving only to protect children until they could care for themselves. In the Boulding vision, the home was a small piece of a new world; it was to be both a harbinger and an agent of peace. The Bouldings thus placed themselves at odds with much contemporary political thought and popular culture. Kenneth and Elise were activists and organizers in local, national, and international contexts. The children felt a certain pressure to "make a contribution"—not the *noblesse oblige* of the Victorian upper class, but a faithful following of the light. Elise Boulding discovered the cost of "undue busyness," even in doing good. Too many speeches, newsletters, articles, meetings, classes, protests, and books—eventually she had to break away from good deeds to be restored in contemplation.

It's harder to measure success in the Bouldings' story than in the McBride Jordan story. Ruth McBride Jordan greatly desired that her children go to college; they all graduated. The Bouldings, both leading academics, desired that their children follow the light, whether or not that led to college. The children took a variety of career paths, all of them internally directed. Just as important, the Bouldings wanted their home to be an encouragement to others (quite unlike the intense privacy of the McBride Jordan family). How many of their live-in students and other guests were moved to be peacemakers? It may be impossible to say. Nevertheless, I think we can fairly say the Bouldings persisted in the pursuit of their vision over several decades.

If Ruth McBride Jordan faced the temptation of despair, the Bouldings faced a temptation to "settle." They had academic success (even fame) and middle-class comfort. Why continue to push so hard to change the world? Who are we to think we can change the world?[23] Against such thoughts, the Bouldings *believed* that their home could be "one small plot of heaven," and they worked creatively to make it so.

---

23. In these rhetorical questions philosophers will hear the voices of ancient stoics and epicureans. The stoic philosophers urged people to accept their assigned roles in life; it didn't matter whether you were a slave or a general, just live according to reason. The epicureans urged people to avoid foolish ambitions—political, economic, etc.—because such striving only caused trouble in the mind. The basic ideas are perennial; without ever reading classical philosophers, many people in our society accept the advice that one should "settle."

8

The Virtue of Religious Faith

I have delayed explicit discussion of religious faith until this chapter for two reasons. First, the central argument of the book—that faith is a virtue because it helps us acquire the internal goods of important practices—is a *moral* argument. Throughout the exploration I have tried to focus mainly on moral questions, though I have made comments on epistemology, political philosophy, and philosophy of science along the way. If I had focused too early on religious faith, it would have only served to confuse things.

Second, when thinking about difficult questions, it often helps to get clear about simpler things before tackling more complex matters. In geometry or logic, we do easy proofs before moving to harder ones. I don't mean to suggest that moral philosophy is simple or easy! But I hope that by this point many readers will agree that faith as described in chapter 2 fits the description of a virtue given in chapter 1. That is, *believing* and *being for* certain things (doubtful things, since one knows that other people do not believe them) really do help people achieve the internal goods of research, reform, and parenting. That faith is a moral virtue, that it is or can be *part of a good life*, seems relatively clear, especially after looking at examples in the previous three chapters.

We have not yet asked whether religious faith is part of a good life—and that question may prove to be more controversial and complicated than the matters explored so far. However, I hope that the foregoing chapters will have prepared the way for our discussion of religious faith, much as the early proofs in geometry and logic clear the way for harder ones.

8.1 IS RELIGIOUS FAITH A VIRTUE?

To one degree or another, evidentialist philosophers judge religious faith to be morally bad, a vice rather than a virtue. The right rule for believing, they say, is to conform one's beliefs and the strength of one's beliefs to the evidence. Religious beliefs routinely violate this rule. For instance, religious people often believe in nonnatural[1] beings (e.g., gods, angels), nonnatural places (e.g., paradise, purgatory), and nonnatural forces or processes (e.g., reincarnation, resurrection). None of these beliefs are supported by evidence, say the evidentialists.[2] To make matters worse, religious people often believe these doctrines with passion and ferocity—they believe much more strongly than the evidence would warrant. The evidentialists clearly believe that these are *moral* failings. As in the case of the shipowner in W. K. Clifford's fable, immoral beliefs can directly harm other people. And even if religious beliefs seem innocuous, like the Catholic belief in transubstantiation, the act of assenting to them inculcates vicious habits of belief in the

---

1. I use the term *nonnatural* rather than *supernatural* to cast my net widely. Historically, the objects of religious belief have varied from group to group, and not every god or divine thing deserves the label *supernatural*.

2. Sometimes an evidentialist will offer a "tidy" argument: the evidence we use in establishing our beliefs must be natural evidence; natural evidence can never support the existence of nonnatural things; therefore belief in nonnatural things can never be right. But in order to work, this argument depends on some definition of "natural" that (1) avoids arguing in a circle and (2) avoids clearly false implications. "Natural" can't just mean "not nonnatural"; that begs the question. Suppose we define "natural" in terms of what the sciences teach us. That would have to include neurobiology and cognitive science. Now, do people have minds? Do other people (other than me) have minds? Do minds exhibit intentional states? Many philosophers hold that minds and intentional states are nonnatural entities or properties. Should we believe in them? A significant school of thought in philosophy of mind, *eliminative materialism*, denies that we should believe in these vestigial bits of "folk psychology." Most naturalistic philosophers writing on such questions admit that it is bizarre to deny the existence of intentional states (what do we say of the person who writes an article to refute folk psychology?), yet they continue to allow that eliminative materialism might be true. It's one of the options in philosophy of mind. Why? Because the naturalistic philosopher is committed to naturalism, and if the nonexistence of intentional mental states is the price of naturalism, so be it.

To escape these problems, the evidentialist might try to offer some other definition of "natural evidence," one that allows minds and intentional states to be real while disallowing gods. No one has succeeded at this yet. Defining "natural" in terms of "physical" doesn't gain anything, since defining "physical" in a non-question-begging and non-absurdity-producing way is just as difficult as defining "natural."

Therefore, in the text I have not supposed that the evidentialist endorses the tidy argument. The evidentialist need not endorse the idea that all evidence must be natural evidence. Whether evidence is natural or nonnatural, the evidentialist says it does not support the religious beliefs mentioned.

persons who hold them. Simon Blackburn says this kind of belief prepares people to believe that other people are witches and ought to be destroyed.

We ought to recognize that a moral protest against religious belief gets some things right. History records ghastly examples of evils perpetrated by religious people who justified their deeds by appeal to religious beliefs, and in some cases the evil deeds were genuinely motivated by religious beliefs. (Sometimes, of course, the religious justifications were merely fig leafs for actions motivated by ordinary lust, greed, hate, or fear.) We cannot deny that at least sometimes *religious faith has helped produce evil*.[3]

Religious believers will object that the religious "faith" that motivated or was used to justify evil actions was deficient in some way. Either the people in question believed things that weren't true or they drew unjustified and immoral conclusions from true doctrines. Religious believers want to say that "true" faith—too often, we just mean "faith like mine"—wouldn't produce such evils.

Superficially, this defense has to be right. A good God would never command or approve of evil. No one really contends that God, if God exists, is other than perfectly good. So on those occasions when believers have thought that God commanded or approved of evil actions, they must have been wrong.

On the other hand, a religious believer would have to be morally obtuse if the consideration of moral evils motivated and justified by religious beliefs did not occasion critical self-examination. Suppose I congratulate myself that I do not share the Aztec's false belief concerning the sun god; I readily see that the Hindu caste system is a vast system of oppression; I repudiate the holy war ideology of the crusades; and so on. Surely my religious beliefs are innocent. *But are they?* Shouldn't the admitted facts of religiously motivated evils—in the past and in today's news—cause me doubt? Stanley Hauerwas, a noted Christian ethicist, has written that every substantive moral doctrine, religious and secular alike, will eventually ask other people to suffer for its commitments.[4] If Hauerwas is even close to being right,

---

3. Even a short list of religiously motivated evils will help make the point. An alphabetical sampling from history: *Aztecs* sacrificed children to feed the sun god; *Buddhists* endorsed the older Hindu caste system; *Christians* persecuted Jews and crusaded against Muslims; *Hindus* practiced suttee (burning a widow alive on her husband's funeral pyre); *Jewish* holy books endorsed genocide (claiming both that ancient Israel carried out genocide and that God punished Israel for failing to carry out genocide); and *Muslims* tried to conquer Europe at various times from the 800s to the 1500s. No doubt, the historical list could be augmented by pulling items from recent newspapers: suicide bombings, wars, destruction of cultural treasures, oppression of aliens, oppression of women, and so on.

4. Hauerwas, *Peaceable Kingdom*, 9.

we ought to hold our moral beliefs with fear and trembling. We're not as innocent as we would like to believe.

I am a Quaker. The Quakers have never killed anybody in God's name—a claim that few religious groups can make. I'm a pacifist, an egalitarian, a humanitarian, and I believe we have a religious duty to protect the environment. Have I found a set of harmless religious beliefs? Not likely. Consider that many moral philosophers reject pacifism, and some of them argue that pacifism harms civil society by undermining its efforts to defend itself against evil. I do not think their arguments are sound, but I am not infallible. If I am wrong about this belief (and I have other beliefs just as controversial), I may in all sincerity of belief do harm to others.

Religious faith *has* contributed to evil. Given human susceptibility to error, the religious believer must admit the *possibility* that his religious faith *will* contribute to evil. But these admissions do not constitute a conclusive moral case against religious faith. Religious faith has also contributed to acts of extraordinary goodness. A moral case against religious faith would have to argue that, all things considered, religious faith was more productive of evil than good. Alternatively, the moral case against religious faith must show that a secular worldview achieves a better balance of good over evil than faith.

Notice that Hauerwas' comment applies to *all* substantive moral doctrines. Secular beliefs might produce and justify evils on par with religiously motivated ones. So, while admitting that evils done in the name of religion should cause us to critically examine our beliefs, religious believers can fairly ask whether religious beliefs are any worse—morally worse—than secular beliefs. Is there any reason to think that religious beliefs are especially pernicious? A secularist might want to say yes, but it would be hard to make the case. Historically speaking, the vast majority of people have been religious believers, so it is hardly persuasive to note that religious believers have perpetrated the bulk of human evil. The twentieth century gives us our best examples of secular societies (admittedly, not exclusively secular); the rise of Hitlerism, Stalinism, Maoism, and the Khmer Rouge does not speak well to the moral superiority of secular societies.

This is where the evidentialists step in. They don't rely on historical argument to condemn religious belief, because they have a philosophical argument. Religious belief is immoral, they say, because it violates the right rule for believing: "It is wrong always, everywhere, and for anyone, to believe anything upon insufficient evidence."[5]

5. The reader will note an irony here. Evidentialists urge us to conform our beliefs to the evidence. The evidence just noted about twentieth-century secular evils would seem to suggest that secular beliefs may be dangerous. Nevertheless, evidentialists

But we have seen that when people believe things upon insufficient evidence those beliefs often help them achieve the internal goods of very important human practices. The evidentialist rule simply fails to recommend itself as a plausible moral guide.[6]

It doesn't seem there is a good moral case *against* religious belief. Is there a *positive* moral argument, an argument based on morality in favor of religious belief?

Many philosophers have said there is.[7] Such arguments typically begin with some feature of morality—that moral laws are real, that morality sometimes requires the individual to sacrifice for others—and then try to show that this feature of morality makes sense if certain religious beliefs are true but is less sensible if the religious beliefs are false. Some of these arguments seem pretty strong. But I will not try to survey or analyze them here.

Is there a positive argument for religious faith within the framework of this book? If we consider religion to be a MacIntyrean practice, could we show that faith serves to help people gain the internal goods of that practice? If we could, then religious faith would be a virtue.

Unfortunately, humanity's religions vary too widely for the argument to work. The religions should be conceived as an array of practices, rather than a single practice. To use Wittgenstein's metaphor, they are like a series of family portraits; some features appear in some religions and not in others. Many religions posit a god or gods, but some don't. Some religions connect morality with religious belief, but some don't. Many hold there is an afterlife, but some don't. No one feature appears in all religions. Some writers on religion have said that all religions offer some version of "salvation," but they hasten to add that salvation is very different in different religions. Some religions say the central human problem is sin; others say it is ignorance; and still others point to other problems. Again, the cure for the human problem varies greatly, whether it is redemption leading to the beatific vision, or enlightenment with the disappearance of all illusion, or something else.

Therefore, I will not try to construct an argument that religious faith, as such, is a virtue. Instead, I will argue that a certain kind of religious faith, my own religious faith, is a virtue. There are two good reasons for focusing on my own beliefs. First, I am more familiar with them than other persons' religious beliefs. Second, I am existentially interested: deciding whether there is a good moral argument for some other faith is far less compelling

---

typically recommend secular beliefs over religious beliefs.

6. Remember, I have no objection to "Advisory Evidentialism." It is often wise to conform one's beliefs to the evidence.

7. For a survey of some moral arguments in support of theism, see Adams, "Moral Arguments for Theistic Belief."

to me than deciding whether there is a good moral argument for my own beliefs.

I do not wish to deny that there may be significant overlap or similarity between my religious beliefs and those of others. I am a Quaker Christian. Almost certainly, then, other Christians will endorse much of what I have to say regarding the internal goods of religion and the role of faith in acquiring them. Adherents of other religions may not endorse all the internal goods of Christian faith—for example, Hindu and Buddhist "hope" will differ from Christian hope—but they may agree with at least some of what follows.

Therefore it is possible that followers of other faiths would endorse the conclusion of my argument, that is, that religious faith is a virtue, because it helps people gain the internal goods of religion. Jews, Christians, and Muslims may all conclude on moral grounds that their religious faith is a virtue. Nothing in the argument I offer prevents this conclusion.

Someone might object that if I admit that (1) Christian faith and Jewish faith are both virtues, (2) that both faiths involve believing certain things, and (3) that some Christian beliefs contradict some Jewish beliefs (for instance, concerning whether God was in Christ Jesus, reconciling the world to himself), then I have simply admitted the incoherence of my position. If the Christian's belief about Jesus is true, then the Jew's belief about Jesus is false; it is not possible that both beliefs could be virtues.

This objection fails to distinguish between practices. As I said above, there are "family resemblances" among the religions, but there is no single common feature to them. Hence, the practice of one religion is not the same thing as the practice of another religion. Remember, I am using "practice" as MacIntyre defined it: "a coherent and complex form of socially established cooperative human activity through which goods internal to that form of activity are realized . . ."[8]

The internal goods of one practice will probably not be the same as the internal goods of another practice, even if the two practices are religions that share many features. Christian faith may be a virtue if it contributes to the internal goods of Christianity. Jewish faith may be a virtue if it contributes to the internal goods of Judaism. There may be overlap between the internal goods of two religions, but presumably there will also be divergence. Notice that in each case I say the religious faith *may* be a virtue. As I said in chapter 1, it is possible for people to be engaged in cooperative human activities that cannot be incorporated into a good life. There may be character traits that conduce to success in such activities without those traits being virtues. Having character traits that enable persons to "succeed" in running a death

8. MacIntyre, *After Virtue*, 187.

camp does not make those character traits virtues, since running a death camp cannot be integrated into a good life.

Nothing in what I have said implies that all religions are true or equally helpful revelations of divine truth. I am not addressing questions of religious pluralism or exclusivism at this time. However, I do claim that if one of the religions is true or significantly closer to the truth than the others, the religious faith of the adherents of the others may still be a moral virtue. Certainly as a Christian I believe that the religious faith of many non-Christians is a moral virtue.

Readers will have anticipated my argument for religious faith:

1. Faith helps one achieve the internal goods of the practice of Christianity.

2. The practice of Christianity, particularly by delivering its internal goods, contributes significantly to a good life.

3. Therefore, Christian faith is a virtue.

Obviously, this argument cries out for elaboration. As I see it, the internal goods of Christianity include at least four goods. We should not think of them as distinct, but as touching each other, interwoven with each other.

First, Christian dogma provides the believer with sufficient intellectual resources to construct a satisfying *worldview*. Such a worldview would allow us to integrate the seemingly disparate elements of our experience in the world. According to biblical creation stories, God created all that exists, and by creating humanity in the divine image God gave human beings an exalted role in the universe. Thus, it is not surprising that a human intellectual creation, mathematics, should prove to be a useful tool in understanding the natural world.[9] According to a Christian worldview, the nature of human beings is such that they should take up the attempt to understand the natural world with an expectation of success.

We believe there remain countless mysteries of the natural world for us to discover. Why should we think that the intellectual capacities of a particular species on an unremarkable planet far out on a spiral arm of a midsized galaxy should be sufficient to gain understanding of the universe? On a purely naturalistic view of human abilities, we should expect that our intellectual capacities have evolved in a random fashion, consistent with natural selection. Of course, the intellectual capacities of every other species have evolved the same way. Why should we believe we have achieved—and will achieve—greater insight into the universe than some

---

9. See Wigner, "Unreasonable Effectiveness of Mathematics in the Natural Sciences."

other species—dolphins, for example?[10] Generally speaking, we *do* think this, and on a Christian worldview, we have good reason to think this.

Besides the starry heavens above, there is the moral law within.[11] On a Christian worldview, it is not surprising that human beings exhibit moral agency. Human beings are able, as Aristotle pointed out, to recognize the difference between pleasure and happiness.[12] So we seek to understand what real happiness is, and why and how virtue is essential to happiness.

On a Christian worldview, it is not surprising that individuals might have moral duties that are incompatible with those individuals' earthly well-being, all things considered. We generally believe that a person may, in some circumstances, have a moral duty the fulfillment of which will compromise her enjoyment of life, or end her life altogether. On a purely naturalistic worldview, such duties are hard to explain, but if there is an afterlife, they make more sense.[13]

In a variety of ways, then, a Christian worldview makes sense of our experience: our belief that the universe is ordered and may be understood, our belief that goodness cannot be reduced to pleasure, and our belief that morality may cost us greatly.

Second, Christian dogma gives the believer a *telos* that organizes morality. "Have this mind in you, which was also in Christ Jesus . . ." says the apostle, urging first-century Christians to imitate Christ's humility and obedience.[14] For Christians, Jesus is in some sense the moral ideal, worthy of admiration and imitation. The implications of Christ's example are by no means clear in every case; Christians struggle to understand their calling and to work it out in practice. For example, while Christians have learned to repudiate the theology of the holy war or crusade, Christians remain divided between pacifism and the theory of the just war.[15] In spite of such debates, the general framework of a Christian's moral life is relatively clear: he has a calling from God to imitate Christ, which means training in virtues

10. In Douglas Adams' delightful science fiction comedies (*The Hitchhiker's Guide to the Galaxy* and others), human beings as a group are among the universe's dolts, while the dolphins are really in the know.

11. Immanuel Kant famously identified the starry heavens and the moral law as two things that stir us to wonder.

12. "Happiness" is the standard translation of *eudaimonia*, but Aristotle meant much more by that word than we usually do by "happiness." Aristotle thought real happiness could only be achieved in *a good life*, considered as a whole. Thus, his witty advice: "count no man happy until he is dead."

13. George Mavrodes makes this argument in "Religion and the Queerness of Morality."

14. Phil 2:5.

15. See Smith, "Integrational Pacifism and the Just War."

such as hope, gentleness, patience, and especially love; and he is a member of a worldwide community of believers, which means solidarity with men and women of every race and ethnic group. The moral life is rightly seen as a life in community, not a lone struggle. Human beings are meant to care for each other, pray for each other, and encourage each other.

Within such a moral framework, a life focused on imitating Christ will still have much room for freedom and creativity. A Christian may find herself torn between life choices of great value—a career in education or in law? Marriage or the single life? Parenthood or devotion to public service?—and by her choices she will create her life, much as an artist creates a sculpture. So we need not worry that the Christian *telos* imposes uniformity upon us. It does, however, make us all pilgrims, people on the way, people striving to become their true selves.

Third, Christian dogma offers the believer *consolation*. The evils of the world, including my sins, do not defeat God. Instead, God overcomes evil by the cross of Christ. God provides forgiveness and grace to the believer, so that the believer may be relieved of guilt and protected from despair.

The "problem of evil" takes up much space in philosophy of religion textbooks. Typical formulations of the problem of evil ask for some explanation of the existence of evil or the sheer quantity of evil or especially horrible evil in the world. If God is good, how is this possible? Rather than add to the vast literature on those questions, I want to consider a different problem of evil. How should we think and act in the light of *the evils we ourselves have done*?

Contemporary moral philosophers don't say much about this problem. They write about moral debates arising from modern life or technology (e.g., is assisted suicide morally permissible?); they debate various conceptions of basic moral terms like *justice*; they analyze virtues and vices; and they sometimes try to convert their audiences to specific moral positions (e.g., Peter Singer thinks we should all be vegetarians). But they don't say much about confronting the evils we have done.[16]

It hardly needs saying that once I recognize that I have done evil, I should stop it. If possible I should make reparations to persons I have hurt. Repentance and restitution—surely these are the proper responses to my "problem of evil." Could it be that moral philosophers say little about the evils we do because little more needs to be said?

---

16. John Kekes criticizes other moral philosophers for neglecting an analysis of evil. Paying more attention to evil, he says, will help us avoid certain mistakes that tend to bedevil liberal democracies. But Kekes focuses on *other* people, evildoers that a wise society must restrain. He doesn't say much about the evils *I* do. See Kekes, *Facing Evil*.

But something more does need to be said. *Despair* is a great danger in the moral life. We resist naming or admitting our sins partly to avoid despair. We tell ourselves, "I only meant it as a joke," "in my family that's how we did things," "it was either us or them," or "I was following orders." We cling tenaciously to such justifications because the alternative seems to be unremitting self-condemnation: "I am a sexist," "I am a child abuser," "I am a warmonger," or "I am a murderer."

We may tell ourselves with Kantian severity that we need to repent and make restitution ("Buck up! You're a rational being, so obey the moral law!"). But without some kind of moral consolation, mere restatements of duty can crush the spirit. *Forgiveness* removes the sting of guilt, and *grace* offers divine help to reform. Pilgrims are more likely to make progress toward their goal if they believe the journey is actually possible. According to Christianity, God offers both forgiveness and grace to human beings.

Fourth, Christian dogma offers the believer the possibility of *hope*. Christians often think of hope in terms of escape from suffering, as if the evils we suffer in this life were the only problem. But the promise of an afterlife opens the door to *sanctification* or *divinization*; that is, the process of being conformed to the character of Christ, begun in this life, can be carried to completion in the next life. Christian dogma allows believers to hope that they actually will become the persons God created them to be. No matter how little of the journey has been completed so far, the Christian pilgrim looks forward with anticipation.

It will be instructive to contrast Christian consolation and hope with the views of a materialist. The ancient Epicureans preached that the good life consisted in the wise pursuit of pleasure. They did not, as their opponents unfairly said, endorse wild parties, because impetuous, short-term pleasure so often leads to long-term regret. Famously, Epicurus said the good life consisted in freedom from "pain in the body and trouble in the mind."[17]

The Epicureans observed that hardly anything causes more "trouble in the mind" than death and religion. People fear death almost as much as they fear what the gods will do to them after they die. The Epicureans thought a single philosophical doctrine could eliminate both fears. They adopted the materialism of Democritus, who taught that all objects were composed of eternal bits of matter so small that they could not be cut (hence "a-toms," from the Greek words for "not cuttable"), and that all changes in the observable world should be understood as rearrangements of the atoms. The upshot of this materialist doctrine, said the Epicureans, is that a human being is precisely and nothing other than a group of atoms. And this provides

17. Jones, *Classical Mind*, 318.

great consolation. "Death is nothing to us," wrote Epicurus, because when a person dies, he simply ceases to exist. The dying person will not experience death, because at that point he no longer experiences anything.

What about the gods? In a passage that speaks to the "problem of evil" as I have described it, Lucretius, a Roman disciple of Epicureanism, asks us to imagine fugitives guilty of serious crimes:

> These same men, exiled from their country and banished far from the sight of men, stained with some foul crime, beset with every kind of care, live on all the same, and, spite of all, to whatever place they come in their misery, they make sacrifice to the dead, and slaughter black cattle and dispatch offerings to the gods of the dead, and in their bitter plight far more keenly turn their hearts to religion. . . . [T]he mask is torn off, and the truth remains behind.[18]

To the Epicurean, suicide is the unspoken but obvious answer to the fugitive's plight. We are asked to imagine a person who has lost the pleasures of human fellowship, whose own conscience causes him great regret, who must always fear being found out by others, and who suffers physical hardships—given all this, the rational thing to do is end the suffering. But, says Lucretius, people irrationally live on, because they fear the gods. *Fear* is the real heart of religion, according to the ancient materialist, and many modern materialists would agree.

Materialism offers consolation once again. Since a person ceases to exist at death, the gods, if they exist, cannot do anything to him after death. Further, in death the guilty fugitive is released from the pangs of conscience.

There is, then, a kind of moral consolation in materialism. Both the evils we suffer and the guilt we endure for what we have done will come to an end. The Christian will say that forgiveness is a better consolation, but the materialist will counter that a true consolation is better than a fictive one.

As I see it, though, materialism offers only a minimal moral hope. Materialism says that as moral beings, we are what accident and our own choices have made us.[19] If our sins tempt us to despair, well, there is nothing for it but to examine the evidence. Many people may rightly conclude that, morally speaking, their lives are beyond repair. Any repair must be self-repair, and it must be accomplished in however many years remain of this

18. Quoted in ibid., 323.

19. Richard Rorty presents this position explicitly, in *Contingency, Irony, and Solidarity*. Rorty contends that our deepest moral commitments come to us largely as historical accidents.

life. Fortunate people can reasonably hope to live moderately good lives, and some exceptional people may achieve saintliness, but moral despair seems quite appropriate for others. Morally speaking, what does material-ism have to offer to people who contributed to genocide? Consider Rwanda in the years 1993–95. Once the madness of the fear and killing ended, some of the killers—perhaps most of them—came to their senses. They realized they were guilty of nothing less than brutal mass murders. On material-ist grounds, should they not consider their lives moral disasters? They can console themselves that one day their existence will end, but can they hope?

To sum up: a person who participates in the practice of Christianity may experience internal goods of that practice, and those goods include a satisfying worldview, a *telos* to admire and pursue, consolation despite the evils we have done, and hope that we will become what we should be. I have focused on these internal goods of Christian practice because they are all relevant to moral living. There may be other goods internal to the practice of Christianity, but the four I have named make it plausible to conclude that the practice of Christianity can contribute to a good life.

Two considerations make it clear that faith greatly helps the Christian achieve these goods. First, the Christian knows plenty of people—rational, well-informed people—who do not believe Christian dogma. They do not believe that God made the world or that God made human beings in the divine image, so they reject the Christian worldview. They may admire some features of Jesus' character, but they do not regard him as a moral ideal. They do not believe in divine forgiveness, and some of them worry that doctrines of forgiveness and grace actually foster moral laziness. They do not believe there is an afterlife, so this-worldly hopes are all we should allow ourselves. The fact that she knows such people gives the Christian *prima facie* grounds to doubt these doctrines. Nevertheless, the Christian *believes* these doctrines, and to the extent that she approves of them, re-joices in them, symbolically endorses them, and the like, she is *for* them. The Christian has *faith*.

Second, it seems clear that faith makes it much more likely that a Chris-tian will acquire the goods I have described. If she doesn't actually admire Jesus, it is unlikely that his example will be the *telos* of her pilgrimage. If she doesn't believe in forgiveness, she probably won't experience forgiveness. And so on. Someone might object that a person can experience God's grace without believing in it; that seems possible. I do not claim that Christian faith is a *necessary condition* for all four internal goods of Christian practice, though it might be for some of them.

It is unfortunately true that there are Christians who miss out on the goods I have described. Perhaps some do not reflect often on God's creation of the world, so they experience it as chaos rather than cosmos. Others, it seems, are so fixated on forgiveness that they care nothing for moral pilgrimage. Still others believe in forgiveness in general, but cannot seem to accept it in their own case. As a result, they struggle with despair.

Given the MacIntyrean framework of this book, I need only claim that Christian faith *tends* to help persons who practice Christianity achieve the internal goods of Christian practice. That seems enough to conclude that Christian faith is a moral virtue, since the internal goods of Christianity contribute to a good life.

8.2 SOME MISCONCEPTIONS ABOUT RELIGIOUS FAITH

In chapter 3, I argued that faith is a virtue. I followed that, in chapter 4, with a discussion of credulity, which is a vice. Many readers may find it easier to agree that faith$_{(8)}$ really is part of good living if it is carefully distinguished from credulity. My project in this section is similar. I have just argued that religious faith is, plausibly, part of good living. Readers may find that conclusion more palatable if religious faith is shorn of certain misconceptions sometimes held by religious people.

Once again, since the religions vary too much to confidently generalize about them, my comments here apply primarily to Christian faith. Adherents of other religions may agree or disagree, depending on the degree of similarity between their religious practice and Christian practice.

Some people, including some Christians, believe that religious faith should be *unfalsifiable*. In the eighteenth century, Gotthold Lessing famously claimed, "Accidental truths of history can never become the proof of necessary truths of reason."[20] Thus, thought Lessing, no historical account, such as the gospels of the New Testament, can serve as an adequate foundation for rational religion. Historically speaking, Lessing helped create liberal Protestant theology, so it might be surprising that some theologically conservative Christians would agree with him. Such persons, liberals and conservatives alike, think that true Christian faith must be safe from any possible counterevidence. They assume, with Lessing, that religious faith ought to be as secure as the "necessary truths of reason."

William Lane Craig shows that Lessing's argument goes wrong in a number of ways.[21] For one thing, contingent truths can serve as proofs of necessary truths, as Saul Kripke pointed out. For example, we discovered

20. Lessing, "On the Proof of Spirit and Power."
21. Craig, "Leaping Lessing's Ugly, Broad Ditch."

that gold has the atomic weight of 69 at a certain time in history; it is an *a posteriori* fact. But that gold has an atomic weight of 69 is a necessary truth; if there is any element with that atomic weight it must be gold, and no element with any other atomic weight can be gold.

More importantly, Lessing's argument goes wrong when it equates religious truths with the truths of reason. We can guess that Lessing had in mind truths of reason such as "2 + 3 = 5" and "if *a* is identical with *b* and *b* is identical with *c*, then *a* is identical with *c*." These truths are certain, and we know them. But what about Goldbach's conjecture, that is, "every even integer greater than 2 can be written as the sum of two primes"? This statement is necessarily true or necessarily false, so one way or the other it is a truth of reason. But we don't know whether it is true or false. Religious believers do not really want a "truth of reason." Religious believers want a comprehensive dogma upon which they can build good lives. They must believe, of course, that the dogma is true; as I said in chapter 2, that's part of what it means to believe something. But Christians don't need a truth that is invulnerable to examination.

Christian dogma makes straightforward historical claims. Jesus was born a Jew under Roman rule, during the reign of Augustus. He was crucified by command of a Roman governor, Pontius Pilate. He rose from the dead the third day. And so on. Christian dogma is historically falsifiable. Believers who desire safety from possible counterevidence long for something very different from what Christianity has to offer.

Possibly, certain historical claims made by Christians could prove to be false without overturning Christian belief in general. The gospel accounts were written some decades after the events they record, based on eyewitness testimony and stories about Jesus handed down among his followers. It would be unsurprising if long-remembered and orally transmitted stories would both record facts and embellish them along the way. An example: the Gospels of Mark and Luke say that Jesus healed a blind man at Jericho; Matthew says he healed two men. Readers can creatively reconcile the details in some way or another, but it would hardly refute Christian doctrine if one or the other account proved inaccurate as to the number of blind men healed at Jericho. On the other hand, if crucial historical claims were shown to be false—for instance those of the Apostles' Creed, mentioned in the previous paragraph—then Christianity is not true.

Besides being historically falsifiable, Christian belief is also *eschatologically* falsifiable. Christian doctrine doesn't tell us nearly as much as we might want to know about the life of the resurrection, but it does rule out some views of the afterlife. If after I die I experience reincarnation rather than resurrection, then that clearly weighs in favor of Hinduism or Buddhism over Christianity. If without resurrection my spirit mingles with the shades of all other dead people, then that would weigh in favor of ancient paganism rather than Christianity, Buddhism, or Hinduism.

Materialists, who believe there is no afterlife, will be frustrated by the whole idea of eschatological falsifiability. It's just an illusion, they will say. What good is a supposed test of a belief that can never be performed? But in the debates between the religions, eschatological falsifiability seems perfectly in order.

Sandra Menssen and Thomas Sullivan have suggested that certain versions of Christian faith are falsifiable in yet another way.[22] The Roman Catholic Church, to a greater degree than many other Christian bodies, has publicly defined certain doctrines. Imagine some future pope convening a Third Vatican Council. If that council were to declare that certain teachings of the church declared to be infallible in prior councils (for instance, the doctrine of transubstantiation that Blackburn condemns), then the teaching of the church would be self-contradictory. Not being a Catholic, I am not committed to this particular doctrine, but Menssen and Sullivan's example shows it is possible that Christian dogma could be falsified by internal contradictions. Indeed, some philosophers have claimed precisely that in regard to the problem of evil: Christian doctrine is necessarily false, they have said, because it combines logically contradictory claims.[23] Christians need to pay attention to such claims and refute them. It won't do to say, "I don't care if my beliefs are logically impossible; I believe them anyway." That would put us in the company of the White Queen.

So much for unfalsifiability. A related misconception is that in regard to Christian faith *evidence is irrelevant*. Some believers think we should not look for or consider evidence for or against the propositions we believe. Real faith, some say, arises only in response to the "word of God" when it is heard. Furthermore, they might say, Jesus chastised Thomas because he desired to see and touch the risen Lord rather than believing on the basis of another's testimony.

But this view is confused. When someone hears the "word of God," whether in a sermon or private conversation, he thereby *has* evidence for the truth of the doctrines presented. In our legal system, we regard *testimony* as a primary category of evidence. And readers of the gospel story (John 20:24–29) should notice that Jesus offered Thomas precisely the evidence he wanted. The point of the story is not to condemn Thomas, but to pronounce

22. Menssen and Sullivan, *Agnostic Inquirer,* 313.

23. Perhaps the classic statement of this argument is Mackie, "Evil and Omnipotence." Needless to say, the debate over the logical problem of evil has gone through many stages since Mackie wrote in 1955.

blessing on those readers of the gospel who did not have Thomas's opportunity to see or touch Jesus. The author of this Gospel is often thought to be
the same person who wrote the letter 1 John, which insists that Christian
teaching is based on something "which we have heard, which we have seen
with our eyes, which we have looked at and our hands have touched" (1
John 1:1).

Having evidence for the things one believes does not remove the
occasion of faith. Remember: in the typical case, faith involves believing
things other people do not believe. In the contemporary world Christians
are familiar with many such people. Their unbelief gives Christians *prima
facie* grounds to doubt. It seems likely that in this world we will always have
need for faith. In heaven, we may speculate, we won't need faith because
then we will *know*. Love, the apostle says, is greater than faith.[24] Perhaps this
is because we will continue to love forever, but we may not always believe
doubtful things.

A third misconception about faith is that *faith precludes doubt*. In the
gospels, Jesus chides his disciples for their fear of a storm (Matt 8:23–27),
and in another story he criticizes Peter's fear of drowning (Matt 14:25–32).
In both stories, Jesus censures a lack of faith, and of Peter he asks, "Why did
you doubt?" On the basis of these stories, some Christians have concluded
that faith and doubt vary inversely: the more faith one has, the less doubt,
and vice versa. Further, they have concluded that to doubt is to sin. Further
still, some have concluded that one can exclude doubt from one's life by an
act of will. One can simply *choose* to believe.

Behind this misconception there is something right, so we have to be
careful in sorting out the confusions. We can get part of the answer by considering voluntary agency. Here I am relying on "folk psychology," so some
philosophers will be immediately skeptical. Nevertheless, most readers will
recognize the following distinctions in their own experience.

We distinguish between involuntary and voluntary bodily actions. I
digest food involuntarily, and I voluntarily walk across the room to fetch
a book. In a roughly similar way, we distinguish between involuntary and
voluntary mental actions. Involuntarily, I hear the sounds of the lawnmower
outside the window (to the extent that it distracts me from something I
would rather think about), and I voluntarily concentrate on writing a gram-
matical sentence.

Believing and doubting are mental activities, and the distinction between voluntary and involuntary actions applies to them. Most of the time
our believing and doubting seems completely involuntary: I see the cat and

24. 1 Cor 13:13.

I believe it is a cat; someone claims a certain beverage will prevent cancer and confer long life, and I am full of doubt. I don't *choose* to believe it is a cat, neither do I *choose* to doubt the bizarre naturopathic medical claim.

Less frequently, we encounter situations in which we seem to have voluntary control over our believing and doubting, if not directly then indirectly. Perhaps it is possible for some people to simply contemplate a proposition—for example, that God was in Christ, reconciling the world to himself—and directly choose to believe it. But that's not the usual way of things. In Clifford's fable of the shipowner, the man did not directly choose to believe that his ship was seaworthy. Instead, he let his mind dwell on a portion of the evidence (the ship had survived storms before, etc.), until he found himself convinced. Surely indirect control of believing and doubting is far more common than believing or doubting by a sheer "act of the will."

Moral philosophers often endorse Kant's dictum "ought implies can." That is, whenever we judge that someone ought to do or have done something, we imply that the person can or could have done it. Put another way: when a person is unable to do something, it seems unjust to condemn her for failing to do it.[25] If we apply "ought implies can" to the distinction between voluntary and involuntary believing and doubting, people would be morally responsible for their voluntary beliefs and doubts.

I suggest, then, that there is a sense in which doubting Christian doctrine can be sinful. A person can voluntarily exercise control over her beliefs (most likely indirectly) in morally vicious ways. Like Clifford's shipowner, she can let her mind dwell on only a portion of the evidence. She can focus her attention on the price to be paid if she were to believe and thus talk herself out of belief. She might unquestioningly "go with the flow" of some social group that rejects Christian belief. And so on. It seems one can sin by doubting.

Having said that, in the normal case doubt is no sin at all. After all, faith, as discussed in chapter 2, involves believing something that is doubtful.

25. I think it is an error to endorse "ought implies can" without qualification. Kant himself concluded that the New Testament, when it apparently commands us to love God and our neighbors, really only commands us to *act as if* we love God and our neighbors. The reason is that we can control our actions, but we cannot control our feelings, what Kant called our "inclinations." It would be unjust for God to command us to do something we cannot do.

Kant's philosophy leads him to obscure the clear meaning of the Old Testament command, which Jesus endorsed: we are to love God with all our heart, and that includes our inclinations.

The command of God, which we cannot directly obey, is nevertheless a command of God. Notice that it directs us to a virtue. It points at the goal toward which we move. To return to the distinction made in the text, we can voluntarily make indirect moves toward obeying the command.

We usually discover that a proposition is doubtful when we meet someone, in person or by reading, who does not believe that proposition. When it comes to religious faith, we are well aware of such people. They are not all uninformed, irrational people. So we are often confronted with *prima facie* reasons not to believe. In the course of thoughtful conversations with such people, Christians may, quite involuntarily, doubt various parts of dogma. When, in the presence of such doubts, we do in fact believe, and we are *for* the things we believe, we have faith.[26] Doubt is not opposed to faith; in the typical case it is part of faith.

It seems we cannot discuss Christian faith without mentioning *trust*. As I said in chapter 1, some virtues seem to require other virtues for their full implementation. Faith in another person often expresses itself as trust. For example, I have faith in my philosophical friends from whom I have solicited feedback on this book. I believe that they are philosophically astute, and I have acted on that belief by asking them to comment on the book. It would be strange if I were to have this faith in them without trusting them to give me honest feedback.

What is true of people is even more true of God. Faith in God should be expressed as trust in God. *Fides* should be expressed in *fiducia*. That is what seems to be lacking in Peter and the other disciples when Jesus chides their lack of faith. They think they believe in Jesus, but when the test comes, they don't trust him. They fear the storm or the water. Of course, the "tests" on the lake were more like quizzes than final exams. According to church tradition, later on Jesus' disciples fared better on tougher tests.

In this matter of believing and doubting, the Christian can exercise some voluntary control. By study, by prayer, by worship—in short, by the traditional avenues of spiritual discipline—the Christian can strengthen his faith. That will mean believing in the presence of doubt, not believing by excluding doubt. And it will be expressed in growing trust in Jesus. We can be confident that for most of us, there will come significant tests of our trust. Only then, in the test, will we know whether we have built up our faith wisely or not.

26. The discussion in the text focuses mostly on *believing* religious doctrines. It would be worthwhile to consider how one can be *for* a religious proposition. For example, how might one be for the fact that God was in Christ, reconciling the world to himself? One might *take comfort* in this doctrine, believing with John Wesley that "even my sins" have been forgiven. One could publicly *affirm* the doctrine, perhaps in conversation with a friend. One could *symbolically stand* for the doctrine, perhaps by joining a Christian church. One could *act politically* on the basis of the doctrine, by opposing political movements that promote division and violence rather than reconciliation.

8.3 ON THE PAIN OF DOUBT

There is a kind of doubt that may be peculiar to religious believers. I speak of the "dark night of the soul." Perhaps the existential angst described by atheist philosophers such as Jean-Paul Sartre or Albert Camus is the same experience wrapped in secular trappings. If so, then unbelief is no more a protection against the pain of doubt than is faith.

The psychological elements of the dark night of the soul are familiar.[27] Early in a believer's pilgrimage, she experiences what she may take to be spiritual normality. In different cases believers' experiences vary. The believer may have visions of divine things; she may "hear" God's voice; she may "feel" God's comfort; and so on. Some philosophers have argued that religious experience, as such, can serve as evidence for the truth of certain religious claims.[28] Whether or not that is true, for the believer this stage of her pilgrimage seems full of light, hope, and cheer. But for many believers the days of light are followed by a night of darkness. Before, God's presence seemed almost palpable, but now he is absent. Before, prayer was a regular, often joyful, part of one's life, but now it seems almost impossible. Before, the truth of Christian doctrines seemed self-evident, but now one doubts God's love, God's promises, and even God's existence.

The believer experiences the dark night of the soul as disappointment, desolation, and extreme loneliness. In short, it hurts to doubt.

Christians' experience of the dark night varies. For Saint John of the Cross, it lasted forty-five years; for others it might last only a week; and still others might never experience it. For some Christians the dark night occurs only once, whereas others go through it repeatedly. The severity of desolation and loneliness experienced probably varies as well. No doubt, secular psychology can theorize about what is "really" going on in the dark night, but no one doubts that the experience, with its characteristic feelings, is quite real. How one interprets the dark night depends on one's worldview.

We could imagine an atheistic argument based on the dark night of the soul:

(1) If a loving God exists, believers would not experience the dark night.

(2) Believers do experience the dark night. Therefore,

(3) God does not exist.

27. The classic text is *Dark Night of the Soul*, from the sixteenth century, by Saint John of the Cross.

28. See Alston, *Perceiving God*.

Philosophers do not seriously offer this argument, because Christian devotional writers from Saint John of the Cross to the present day consistently reject the first premise. They say that God *gives* the dark night to the believer precisely because God loves the believer. The dark night purges the soul of its reliance on feelings, leading to a deeper faith.

While the imagined atheistic argument of the previous paragraph is a nonstarter, some Christians may worry about a much more personal argument. In the midst of the dark night, the believer may doubt whether he is, in fact, a Christian. Some Christians associate their faith so closely with certain feelings that they may think the absence of those feelings proves that they have no faith. If we put this worry in argument form, it would look like this:

> (4) At times in the past I had faith and I experienced certain feelings, including a feeling of certainty about Christian doctrines.

> (5) I do not now experience those feelings; in particular, I feel doubt about Christian doctrines.

> (6) Therefore, I must no longer have faith.

Premises (4) and (5) may be true, but the argument is invalid. To make the argument valid, we need to replace premise (4) with something like this: (7) Because having faith has been associated with certain feelings, including a feeling of certainty about Christian doctrines, having faith will always be associated with those feelings.

We have no reason to think (7) is true. To the contrary, Scripture records many cases of faithful people who experienced a wide variety of feelings, including feelings of loneliness and desolation. Think of the psalms, the book of Job, or Christ's prayer in the garden on the night of his arrest.

Nevertheless, the worry may not die easily. Maybe some negative feelings, such as loneliness or depression, can be combined with faith, but can a person have *doubt* and *faith* at the same time? Yes.

Once again we need to pay attention to folk psychology. We can all recognize the difference between what philosophers call *dispositional* and *occurrent* mental states. This distinction applies to emotions and intentions as well as beliefs. An occurrent mental state is what it sounds like: it is what a person is currently doing, feeling, or intending. A dispositional mental state is one that is not currently active in a person's consciousness, but that will become conscious if the person is properly stimulated. For example, I love my wife. Happily, I often have occasions in which I am conscious of this fact—I buy her flowers, tell her that I love her, hold hands with her, etc. On these sorts of occasions I may be said to love my wife occurrently. At other times—when I am asleep, while concentrating on a philosophy problem, while playing softball, etc.—I am not conscious of my wife at all. It would be silly to say that I do *not* love my wife, even at those times when, as we say, she is the furthest thing from my mind. Rather, we should say that I love my wife dispositionally. Given the proper stimulation, my dispositional love for my wife will become occurrent.

If we reflect on the difference between dispositional and occurrent mental states, we find resolution for apparent conundrums. Imagine two business partners, Bill and Bob. Bill manages production in their factory while Bob sells their product, often traveling to distant cities to meet clients. Bill trusts Bob to be a good partner, in particular by not frivolously spending company money while on the road. Bill's trust in Bob is almost always dispositional rather than occurrent. He very rarely thinks about it. But then Bill hears a report that Bob was seen hosting possible clients at a sleazy bar in Las Vegas. The report shocks Bill, and it causes him doubt. Does he trust Bob anymore? The answer is that Bill trusts (dispositionally) while he also doubts (occurrently).

Bill will certainly find this conflict between his dispositional and occurrent mental states unsettling. He will do something to resolve it, and this may be as simple as picking up the phone and getting Bob's report on the situation. But we can imagine cases in which the resolution of such conflicts could take a long time, requiring a person to live in the tension between dispositional faith and occurrent doubt for an extended period. Maybe Bob is shot by a mugger, and he suffers brain damage and loss of memory. Neither Bill nor Bob can obtain good evidence for why Bob was in the bar.

Christians sometimes doubt Christian doctrines, doubting even that God exists. The dark night of the soul is painful. But doubt and pain do not prove the absence of faith. Instead, the Christian may have dispositional faith combined with occurrent doubt. The Christian's form of life may express his dispositional faith, that is, he continues to act in ways consistent with faith. He prays, he participates in public worship, he works for social justice, and he continues a moral pilgrimage focused on the example of Jesus. All the while, he may experience occurrent doubt.

It is possible, of course, that the experience of occurrent doubt will provoke a crisis in the Christian's life. He may abandon his prior form of life based on faith. He may give up Christian hope and repudiate Christian moral pilgrimage. In such a case, the conflict between dispositional faith and occurrent doubt is resolved by abandoning faith.

In a happier case (here I mean "happy" in Thomas Aquinas' sense of *eudaimonia* directed toward our supernatural end), the Christian resolves the tension between dispositional faith and occurrent doubt by means of *patience.* No doubt, he prays for consolation and joy, for return to the days of light. But as long as the dark night continues, he continues to pray and wait.

8.4 SUMMARY: THE VIRTUE OF RELIGIOUS FAITH

Religious faith can be vicious.[29] But since the world's religions constitute different practices, it is possible that some instances of religious faith can be virtuous. In the framework of this book, religious faith would be a virtue if it tended to help persons achieve the internal goods of the religion, with the proviso that the practice of the religion can be integrated into a good life. In this chapter I have argued that Christian faith meets this standard, since it contributes to four important and morally positive internal goods of Christianity: a satisfying worldview, a *telos* to pursue, moral consolation, and moral hope.

Other examples of religious faith may also be virtues. Without examining particulars, I presume that this is true in many cases.

Christian faith ought not to be confused with unfalsifiability. Christian believers ought to be ready to examine evidence for and against their beliefs. Christian believers ought not to be surprised if they experience doubt, since faith typically coexists with doubt. Christians should not be surprised if their doubts bring experiences of desolation and loneliness. The "dark night of the soul" does not mean that the Christian has lost faith, nor will it prevent the Christian's faith from producing the internal goods of Christianity mentioned above.

Therefore, on moral grounds, at least some instances of religious faith should be regarded as virtuous: an acquired characteristic of a person which tends to enable the person to achieve the internal goods of a practice that can be integrated into a good life.

29. I focus on the faith of the individual believer, not the various religions, though they are sometimes called "faiths."

Bibliography

Adams, Robert M. *Finite and Infinite Goods: A Framework for Ethics*. Oxford: Oxford University Press, 1999.

————. "Moral Arguments for Theistic Belief." In *The Virtue of Faith and Other Essays in Philosophical Theology*, 144–63. Oxford: Oxford University Press, 1987.

————. *A Theory of Virtue: Excellence in Being for the Good*. Oxford: Oxford University Press, 2006.

Allen, Nick. *The Cepheid Distance Scale: A History*. www.institute-of-brilliant-failures.com.

Alston, William. *Perceiving God: The Epistemology of Religious Experience*. Ithaca: Cornell University Press, 1991.

Blackburn, Simon. *Truth: A Guide*. Oxford: Oxford University Press, 2005.

Blanshard, Brand. *Reason and Belief*. New Haven: Yale University Press, 1975.

Boghossian, Peter. "Faith, Belief and Hope: From Cognitive Sickness to Moral Virtue and Back Again." Public talk at Portland State University, November 17, 2011.

Boulding, Elise. *One Small Plot of Heaven: Reflections on Family Life by a Quaker Sociologist*. Wallingford, PA: Pendle Hill, 1989.

Brendlinger, Irv. *Social Justice Through the Eyes of Wesley: John Wesley's Theological Challenge to Slavery*. Guelph, ON: Joshua Press, 2006.

Carroll, Lewis. *Alice's Adventures in Wonderland & Through the Looking Glass*. New York: Signet Classics, 1960.

Clifford, W. K. "The Ethics of Belief." In *Lectures and Essays*, edited by Leslie Stephen and Frederick Pollock, 339–63. London: Macmillan, 1886. Online: people.brandeis.edu/~teuber/Clifford_ethics.pdf.

Coles, Robert. *Dorothy Day: A Radical Devotion*. Reading, MA: Addison-Wesley, 1987.

Craig, William L. "Leaping Lessing's Ugly, Broad Ditch." www.reasonablefaith.org/site/News2?page=NewsArticle&id=5735.

Day, Dorothy. *The Long Loneliness*. New York: Harper & Row, 1952.

Fendall, Lon. *To Live Free: William Wilberforce—Experiencing the Man, the Mission, and the Legacy*. Uhrichsville, OH: Barbour, 2007.

Foot, Philippa. "Virtues and Vices." In *Virtue Ethics*, edited by Roger Crisp and Michael Slote, 163–77. Oxford: Oxford University Press, 1997.

Forrest, Jim. *Love Is the Measure: A Biography of Dorothy Day*. Maryknoll, NY: Orbis, 1986.

Gettier, Edmund. "Is Justified True Belief Knowledge?" *Analysis* 23 (1963) 121–23.

Grindlay, Jonathan E., et al. "Digitizing the Harvard College Observatory Plate Collection: An Instrument for the 'Historic Sky.'" http://tdc-www.harvard.edu/plates/presentations/USNO2005.pdf.

Harvard Astrographic Plates. Online: http://tdc-www.harvard.edu/plates/presentations/USNO2005.pdf.

Hauerwas, Stanley. *The Peaceable Kingdom: A Primer in Christian Ethics*. Notre Dame: University of Notre Dame Press, 1983.

Herbert, Robert T. "Is Coming to Believe in God Reasonable or Unreasonable?" *Faith and Philosophy* 8 (1991) 36–50.

Holmes, Arthur F. *The Idea of a Christian College*. Rev. ed. Grand Rapids: Eerdmans, 1987.

Hume, David. *A Treatise of Human Nature*. In *The Essential David Hume*, edited by Robert Paul Wolff, 23–154. New York: New American Library, 1969.

Johnson, George. *Miss Leavitt's Stars: The Untold Story of the Woman Who Discovered How to Measure the Universe*. New York: Norton, 2005.

Jones, W. T. *A History of Western Philosophy*. Vol. 1, *The Classical Mind*. 2nd ed. New York: Harcourt Brace Jovanovich, 1970.

Kekes, John. *Facing Evil*. Princeton: Princeton University Press, 1990.

Lakoff, George, and Mark Johnson. *Metaphors We Live By*. Chicago: University of Chicago Press, 1980.

———. *Philosophy in the Flesh: The Embodied Mind and Its Challenge to Western Thought*. New York: Basic Books, 1999.

Leavitt, Henrietta. "1777 Variables in the Magellanic Clouds." *Annals of the Astronomical Observatory of Harvard College* 60.4 (1908) 87–108.

———. "Periods of 25 Variable Stars in the Small Magellanic Cloud." *Harvard College Observatory Circular* 173 (1912) 1–3.

Lessing, Gotthold. "On the Proof of Spirit and Power" (1777). faculty.tcu.edu/grant/hhit/Lessing.pdf.

Lewis, C. S. *Mere Christianity*. New York: Macmillan, 1943.

MacIntyre, Alasdair. *After Virtue*. Notre Dame: University of Notre Dame Press, 1981.

———. *Dependent Rational Animals*. Chicago: Open Court, 1999.

Mackie, J. L. "Evil and Omnipotence." *Mind* 64 (1955) 200–12.

Mavrodes, George. "Religion and the Queerness of Morality." In *God*, edited by Timothy Robinson, 74–89. 2nd ed. Indianapolis: Hackett, 2002.

McBride, James. *The Color of Water: A Black Man's Tribute to His White Mother*. New York: Riverhead, 1996.

McCoy, Roger M. *Ending in Ice: The Revolutionary Idea and Tragic Expedition of Alfred Wegener*. Oxford: Oxford University Press, 2006.

Meek, Esther Lightcap. *Loving to Know*. Eugene, OR: Cascade Books, 2011.

———. "Michael Polanyi and Alvin Plantinga." *Philosophia Christi* 14 (2012) 57–77.

Menssen, Sandra, and Thomas D. Sullivan. *The Agnostic Inquirer: Revelation from a Philosophical Standpoint*. Grand Rapids: Eerdmans, 2007.

Metaxas, Eric. *Amazing Grace: William Wilberforce and the Heroic Campaign to End Slavery*. San Francisco: HarperSanFrancisco, 2006.

Morrison, Mary L. *Elise Boulding: A Life in the Cause of Peace*. Jefferson, NC: McFarland, 2005.

Murdoch, Iris. *Metaphysics as a Guide to Morals*. London: Chatto & Windus, 1992.

———. *The Sovereignty of Good*. London: Routledge & Kegan Paul, 1970.

Neiman, Susan. *Evil in Modern Thought.* Princeton: Princeton University Press, 2004.

Nietzsche, Friedrich. *The Genealogy of Morals.* 1887. Online: www2.southeastern.edu/ Academics/. . ./nietzschegenealogy.pdf .

Plantinga, Alvin. "Reason and Belief in God." In *The Analytic Theist*, edited by James F. Sennett, 102–61. Grand Rapids: Eerdmans, 1998.

Pojman, Louis. "Faith, Hope and Doubt." In *Philosophy of Religion: An Anthology*, edited by Louis Pojman and Michael Rea, 412–22. 5th ed. Belmont, CA: Thompson/ Wadsworth, 2008.

Rachels, James. *The Elements of Moral Philosophy.* New York: Random House, 1986.

Roberts, Robert C., and W. Jay Wood. *Intellectual Virtues: An Essay in Regulative Epistemology.* Oxford: Oxford University Press, 2007.

Rorty, Richard. *Contingency, Irony, and Solidarity.* Cambridge: Cambridge University Press, 1989.

Russell, Bertrand. "Why I Am Not a Christian." In *Why I Am Not a Christian, and Other Essays on Religion and Related Subjects*, 3–23. London: Allen & Unwin, 1957. http://www.users.drew.edu/~jlenz/whynot.html

Smith, Philip. "Integrational Pacifism and the Just War." In *Pazifismus: Ideengeschichte, Theorie und Praxis*, edited by Barbara Bleisch and Jean-Daniel Strub, 163–76. Bern: Haupt, 2006.

———. *The Virtue of Civility in the Practice of Politics.* Lanham, MD: University Press of America, 2002.

Wallace, James. *Virtues and Vices.* Ithaca: Cornell University Press, 1978.

Wegener, Alfred. *The Origins of Continents and Oceans.* Translated by John Biram. 4th ed. New York: Dover, 1966.

———. *Tagebücher, Briefe, Erinnerungen.* Compiled by Else Wegener. Wiesbaden: Brockhaus, 1960.

Widdows, Heather. *The Moral Vision of Iris Murdoch.* Aldershot, UK: Ashgate, 2005.

Wigner, Eugene. "The Unreasonable Effectiveness of Mathematics in the Natural Sciences." *Communications in Pure and Applied Mathematics* 13 (1960) 1–14.

Wittgenstein, Ludwig. *On Certainty.* New York: Harper & Row, 1969.

———. *Philosophical Investigations.* New York: Macmillan, 1953.

———. *Preliminary Studies for the "Philosophical Investigations," Generally Known as the Blue and Brown Books.* New York: Harper, 1958.

Wood, W. Jay. "Faith's Intellectual Rewards." Paper presented at the Pacific/Mountain Region Conference of the Society of Christian Philosophers, George Fox University, Newberg, Oregon, March 2011.

Zagzebski, Linda. *Virtues of the Mind.* Cambridge: Cambridge University Press, 1996.

Index